"ALWAYS LIVE BETTER THAN YOUR CLIENTS"

OTHER BOOKS BY ISADORE BARMASH

Nonfiction
*More than They Bargained for—the Rise and Fall of Kor-
vettes*
The Chief Executives
For the Good of the Company
The World Is Full of It
Welcome to Our Conglomerate—You're Fired!
The Self-Made Man

Fiction
Net Net

Anthology
Great Business Disasters

Benjamin Sonnenberg

"ALWAYS LIVE BETTER THAN YOUR CLIENTS"

The Fabulous Life
and Times of
Benjamin Sonnenberg,
America's Greatest
Publicist

Isadore Barmash

DODD, MEAD & COMPANY · NEW YORK

Copyright © 1983 by Isadore Barmash
All rights reserved
No part of this book may be reproduced in any form
without permission in writing from the publisher
Published by Dodd, Mead & Company, Inc.
79 Madison Avenue, New York, N.Y. 10016
Distributed in Canada by
McClelland and Stewart Limited, Toronto
Manufactured in the United States of America
Designed by Jennie Nichols/Levavi & Levavi

First Edition

Library of Congress Cataloging in Publication Data

Barmash, Isadore.
  "Always live better than your clients."

  Bibliography: p.
  Includes index.
  1. Sonnenberg, Benjamin, 1901– . 2. Press agents—
United States—Biography. I. Title.
HM263.S633B37 1983   659.2'092'4 [B]   83-9078
ISBN 0-396-08216-5

The excerpts on pages 180, 181, 343, 344 from *Merchant Princes* by Leon
Harris, Copyright © 1979 by Leon Harris, are reprinted by permission of
Harper & Row, Publishers, Inc.

Grateful acknowledgment is made to *The Nation* and to *Grand Street* for
permission to quote from "Lost Property," Copyright © 1979, 1980, 1982
by Ben Sonnenberg.

The excerpts on pages 789–90 from *The Nation* of June 30, 1979 are Copyright © 1979 Nation Magazine, The Nation Associates, Inc. Reprinted by
permission.

Excerpts from *The New Yorker* copyright © 1950, 1978 The New Yorker
Magazine, Inc. Reprinted by permission.

TO ALL THOSE
WHO SHARED IN THE
ADVENTURE
OF PIERCING THE ENIGMA

CONTENTS

·ix·

FOREWORD

This is a book that was not supposed to be.

In his consummately persuasive way, Benjamin Sonnenberg convinced the members of his family, some of his closest friends, and some of his clients that he did not care to have a biography, that all his personal papers and professional files were to be destroyed on his death, and he left them with the conviction that they were not to discuss him publicly afterward.

"Ben wanted to be remembered as he was in his prime," said Brendan Gill, the noted writer and drama critic of *The New Yorker*. "A biography would have raked up the past, the poverty and the struggling and he wanted to forget that." And that was all that Gill, one of the closest in the Sonnenberg inner circle, would say.

But there are enough others who associated with, worked

with, and visited Sonnenberg in his famous Gramercy Park mansion that much can be told. Manifestly despite the reluctance of those "sworn" to secrecy, the life of this man—considered America's greatest publicist; a highly influential adviser to the nation's most important businessmen and politicians; one of the world's great collectors of art and antiques; a host to the great, royal, cultured and talented; and, perhaps, above all, a deliberately contrived and beloved eccentric—should be narrated.

Whether Sonnenberg's reluctance was indeed because he wanted to be remembered only in his prime is another matter. His demand for posthumous anonymity was mystifying, paradoxical, even feisty, considering that he sold and thrived on publicity. Perhaps he hoped that his legend would only grow with time, its edges blurring but its core enriching itself, vermeiled by nostalgia. Or perhaps he just didn't want anyone raking over the hot coals that he had lit in his long, controversial career.

This book will be an attempt to get behind the legend, to present in a full, realistic way a very unusual man and personality. He achieved an ideal that many seek and few attain. He decided early, before he was fifteen years old, exactly what he wanted to be, how he would be perceived, and then he devoted the next sixty years to accomplishing the ideal and succeeded in every way. He even tried to preserve it after death by keeping the foisted image the way he wanted it to be, not allowing an outsider to tamper with it.

Primary acknowledgment must go to Freya Manston, the literary agent who originated the idea for this book; also to Jerry Gross, my editor at Dodd, Mead, and Lewis Gillenson, its President, for their interest and support. My deep gratitude also goes to John Scott Fones, James Bowling, Frank Saunders, Alistair Cooke, Theodore Kheel, Denny Griswold, Frank Weil, Gershon Kekst, Brooke Astor, Herbert Rowland, Stanley Marcus, William Tobey, William Ruder, Andrew Goodman, Irving Straus, Robert E. Bedingfield, Carl Spielvogel, Edward Munves Sr., Edward Munves Jr., Leonard Matt, Jay Scott, Ray Josephs, Jerry Berns, Bert Behrens, Warren Owens, Julian Bach, Pete Kriendler, and Sheldon Kriendler.

As to those people who could have helped but didn't, for

whatever their reasons, I hope that as they read this work—and I believe they will—they will regret their reluctance. Ben deserved a biography, with halo and warts, whether he wanted one or not.

BOOK
ONE

1

"I'VE BECOME VERY ADROIT AT THIS THING"

Early in 1978, the happy, plump, little man, his normal paleness turned to gray, became seriously ill. But, in June, he roused himself. With the help of his valet, he dressed carefully, had his suitcases packed, and was driven in a hired, black limousine to the airport, where he departed for the great antiques auction in London. He bought a few pieces there and shortly afterward flew home to his bed.

In September, Brendan Gill, the drama critic for *The New Yorker*, told a friend, "I got in to see him. You should have seen it. He got himself all done up. He had put on his robe and his scarf. He was the same as ever, except that you could tell he was not quite right but he was as witty as ever. When I asked him why he had gone to the London antiques show, he said he had to because it was the biggest one in years. And not only that but he had bought a few things."

"But he was dying," the friend said.

Gill shrugged. "It's not strange as you might think," he said. "It was a last stab at being alive. To a collector, buying is living."

A few days later, on September 6, Benjamin Sonnenberg was dead. He was seventy-seven, exceeding the biblical life span by several years. But, spurred by an immense joie de vivre, which had few parallels in the broad, middle decades of the twentieth century, he had led six, separate lives, each one of which would have sustained a legend. He was the era's premiere publicist. He was an invaluable consultant to the elite of American business. He was a social counselor to the rich, helping to inject meaning into aimless if well-padded lives. He was one of the time's greatest collectors of art, sculpture, and brass. As a host extraordinaire, his famous mansion on Gramercy Park was one of the most popular and busiest centers for the ingathering of the famous, the talented, and the celebrated. And as a bon vivant, he was known in the great restaurants, hotels, watering places, and inns of the Western world.

But, above all, perhaps, he was the apostle of style, of grace, of a life style that had all but vanished. He was, admittedly, hard to take, with his flamboyant dress, his ornate home, and his fanciful, convoluted manner of speaking. But he was also hard to forget. And though he created his own image of superior taste and affluence, he was accepted as an authentic by the famous, the rich, and the powerful. He accepted his successful, self-marketing as only his due. But those who knew him best, who saw him most often, couldn't help noticing the twinkle that hung back, but not too far, in his eyes. He was putting something over, having a hell of a time with it, and it lasted a long time.

For many years, from the 1940s through the 1970s, he was a familiar, somewhat arcane figure. Strolling along Fifth Avenue, past Rockefeller Center, the great stores, St. Patrick's Cathedral, and then along Fifty-seventh Street's myriad art galleries, where he was one of the most welcomed customers, he presented one of those irrepressible sights that made New Yorkers' and tourists' hearts beat faster and their eyes pop. A small, rotund man, whose walrus mustache seemed incongruous in a cherub's face, he always wore a black homburg, a chesterfield, and spats and swung a cane. He was a dandy out of an Oscar Wilde play amid the sea of trenchcoats and three-piece suits. People just stopped and stared at the dapper but rather antiquated figure on the better streets of New York, London, and Paris, perhaps because he remained an Edwardian anachronism in an era of plastic, pop art, and pizza. He smiled back, obviously enjoying the curiosity, but he remained reserved and indomitable. Graciousness endured, he implied, as long as he did. Often, with a benign but shrewd smile, he would dart into a Manhattan gallery or stop to chat happily with an acquaintance, more than likely one of the city's elite. And always the long, black limousine that trailed him along the curb in case he got tired (although he seldom did) would stop, too, and wait.

He could have been some tycoon's English butler, an august maitre d', an international impresario, a duke or baron, a renowned art dealer, or a self-made millionaire indulging his idiosyncrasies. Or he could have been the real-life personification of the little man on the cover of *Esquire* magazine. Actually, Ben Sonnenberg was a little of each—a feisty, bubbling mixture whose personal and professional life created an American legend in those broad, middle years of the twentieth century.

In the late afternoons and especially in the evenings at his thirty-seven-room house at 19 Gramercy Park South in Manhattan, he really came into his own—as an alchemist of people. There, in what critics considered one of the last, great, private mansions, he would entertain some of the world's best-known celebrities and some talented or charismatic people still unknown but with much potential. Business clients, many of them multimillionaires, would stare in disbelief as his butler, Leonard Horn, welcomed them, opening a great, black door with brass lion's-head knocker, and preceded them up several stairways lined with fine collections of antiques, paintings, sculpture, and brass, many clearly of the first rank. In the vast, paneled library, they would have met in an earlier era, Samuel Goldwyn, Somerset Maugham, Ernest Hemingway, and John O'Hara; and in a later era, William S. Paley, Henry Kissinger, and Norman Mailer. And, eventually they would meet

Ben Sonnenberg himself, who would finally come forward with an outstretched hand. His theory was rub people together and great sparks would fly.

It was in the mornings and early afternoons, however, that Sonnenberg plowed and seeded in the field in which he became the best-known American practitioner, a Benvenuto Cellini of the corporate image. He sought out the vein of gold under the skin of the businessman, and if it wasn't to be found Sonnenberg gold-plated him.

From his early career as a show-business and night-club press agent, he realized that dignified glamor could gloss over otherwise mundane corporate chiefs. He exposed Charles Luckman, a moderately well-known architect, to the top writers and newspapermen in the country, counseled him on art, and later on marketing techniques when Luckman became president of Lever Brothers. In a few years, he had Luckman on the cover of *Time* magazine. Some years later, though, when Luckman's star had receded and he complained that Sonnenberg had let him down, the publicist replied, with some asperity, "I put you where you are. If you can't stay up there, that's your fault, not mine." He told Arthur Genet, the chairman of the Greyhound Corporation, that Genet needed to personalize himself and his company. So at Sonnenberg's suggestion, Genet turned one of his superbuses into a lush, mobile sitting room in which he visited the various Greyhound offices and terminals, inviting into the comfortable interior not only his employees but the public as well. Incidentally, when Genet first came to New York to visit him, Sonnenberg was visibly startled by the visitor's black-and-white shoes. "Arthur," he said, "in the boondocks you can wear footwear with black and white. In New York City, we wear shoes of only one color. Either black or brown."

Sonnenberg's Broadway background taught him that people tend to react with surprise in two ways: they are genuinely impressed by impressive situations, or they are impressed only after they see that others are. Both these principles—which proved themselves by peoples' reactions to his lavish home; his seven live-in servants; the amazing cleanliness, shine, and sparkle of his possessions; the great art collection; and his instruction to the owners of some of the better restaurants that whenever he received a telephone call a busboy was to look for him at a number of tables so that his presence would be widely known—permeated both his personal and professional life.

"Always live better than your clients," he would advise his publicist contemporaries and his small staff, most of whom couldn't possibly have afforded it. But he knew there was nothing as effective as the impact of a sense of heightened anticipation. That's why he saw to it that a client or a prospective client had to make that long trek at 19 Gramercy Park before he, the host, appeared. Who would not quail at passing through an outer vestibule, an inner hall, across one room, up the stairs or in an elevator, through another room, all the time peering at hundreds of pieces of art and artifacts before entering the awesome living room or library? He kept a fifty-seat projection room on the fifth floor for advance showing, prior to commercial release, of major, new movies. His friendship with Sam Goldwyn, of course, helped him in that connection. Why shouldn't Goldwyn, who had a legendary ability to mangle the English language, be grateful? Sonnenberg couldn't help boasting, nor for that matter could Goldwyn, of the fact that the publicist had turned the movie tycoon into a speaker who received a standing ovation at Oxford University.

That turnabout may be astonishing in itself. But there are some indications that Sonnenberg, whose mind had a pixyish turn, had engineered a double twist in the case of Goldwyn. Approached by the movie maker to help him overcome "a couple of minor, severe problems," Sonnenberg quickly put Goldwyn in the hands of a speech expert to give him a greater credibility with bankers and critics. But just to keep Sam's unique way with language an important element in Goldwyn's picaresque personality, Sonnenberg encouraged him to speak naturally in less sophisticated circles. Perhaps it is true that contrasts imbue the total product with a greater tang, like mustard on cheese or steak tartare and milk shakes.

Sonnenberg, of course, knew the impact of bait on a tenuous hook, of that heightening anticipation when a desirable target seems a bit out of reach. He instructed his friends that he was not to be considered easy to get. And that was how Goldwyn became so eager to have Sonnenberg handle him.

When Goldwyn approached Albert Lasker, the Chicago advertising man who was considered to be at the top of the profession, and asked for advice on his image problems, Lasker replied, "Sam, you really have problems. There's really only one guy who can help you. But, number one, he wouldn't touch a guy like you and, number two, you couldn't afford him if he would."

"Who the hell is it?" Goldwyn asked.

"Ben Sonnenberg, the best public-relations man in America."

Goldwyn immediately flew to New York. A week later, Sonnenberg went to work for Goldwyn.

But if Ben could be both puckish and determined, he indulged the combination to startle a client into some unusual introspection of his own hardheaded behavior.

In the late 1960s, W. Maxey Jarman, chairman of Genesco, Inc., formerly the General Shoe Company, came to Sonnenberg for some advice. Jarman had become a controversial figure in American business because of his penchant for acquiring, sometimes raiding, one company after another. Now Genesco was being drained by declining profits, principally because of several ill-advised acquisitions and Jarman's unbending opposition to criticism. In a few weeks, he would face certain, stormy complaints from irate, large shareholders at the annual meeting in Nashville. "I'd love to divert the attention of the shareholders," said Jarman, "and blunt their complaints. What should I do?"

It was time for some ridiculous advice, Ben surmised, to give Jarman the balance the wheeler-dealer sorely needed.

Sonnenberg knew that, in addition to Jarman's hunger for empire building, the entrepreneur was something of a showman. He told Jarman, "Why don't you hire a bunch of chorus girls and put on a show at the meeting?"

Jarman nodded nervously. "Yes, yes," he said, "but what should I do about my profits?"

"Stop issuing quarterly financial reports. That ought to help."

Jarman swallowed painfully. "The S.E.C. might not like it, but we might get away with it for a while. But what the hell should I do about my board of directors? They're starting to give me trouble, too."

Sonnenberg took a few long sips of tea from his glass and then said, "Fire the whole bunch, one by one. Then go outside, preferably to Fifth Avenue, and hire the first ten men you meet, no matter who they are. That ought to end your troubles with the board."

As Jarman staggered out, Sonnenberg added, "Just a minute. To show you how confident I am that it will all work, I'll wager my fee on it."

Jarman paid the handsome fee, but didn't follow any of the suggestions. He did, however, try a ruse of his own: he sent word back from Nashville that the plan didn't work. But Sonnenberg, not one to be easily outwitted, never returned the fee, probably on the basis that the soundness of his counsel had not been tested because Jarman had not put it to work.

Sonnenberg, in fact, believed in high fees for his services and usually got them. As William Tobey, the former senior vice-president for sales promotion of Abraham and Straus, the Brooklyn department store, recalls, "When our management asked me to approach Sonnenberg to get his help, he asked what fee we had in mind. I named a figure that seemed right, but Sonnenberg said, 'For that kind of fee, I do not even unzip my fly.' "

His demand for a high reward for his services was as much part of his nature as his flamboyant dress. Although he rose from poverty, he believed enthusiastically in his worth, his superiority over the men whom he served, and in his grandiose way of life. He once explained why he was New York's most energetic host. "I resolved to become a cross between Condé Nast and Otto Kahn," referring to the famous fashion magazine publisher and the internationally known banker and patron of the arts, both among the great hosts of their time. On why he chose to handle only chief executives of major corporations, he said, "I deal only with head men and in general confine myself to corporations rather than individuals." He added, "I deal mostly with hundred-thousand-a-year men, and when they come to my house, they know that I make more than that myself."

Nonetheless, his eyes would widen when he met for the first time someone truly important or a celebrity on the rise. If the twinkle in his eye and his occasional capriciousness denoted that he didn't take it all very seriously, he still felt that nothing generated success as much as connections with people in high places. This contact with the powerful in business, finance, government, and the arts provided what he called "the levers of power." And though he appeared at times obsessed with pulling those levers, he preferred to do it from a distance. He liked to put people together to see what would happen while standing off just a bit from it. He sensed that the king maker might really have more clout than the king, but just as likely he simply enjoyed the alchemy he performed. He himself never felt that he could write very well, despite all his years in the publicity field. But he was a great fan of any new writing that pleased him and that was how I met him.

On a late afternoon in 1969, my office phone rang and a warm, paternal voice said, "This is Ben Sonnenberg. Your new book, *The Self-Made Man*, has created a stir. I have bought twenty-four copies, which I am sending to friends. I do this sort of thing when an important, new book comes out. No, don't thank me, please. It's not necessary. How would you like to have tea with me tomorrow at six?"

Had he "bought" the books? Or did he have an arrangement with the promotion department of my publisher, as well as that of various other publishers, to receive gratis copies of forthcoming titles, which he could then send to his clients? It was probably, I concluded, just the sort of thought a jaded newspaperman would have about a P.R. man. Later I learned that he had a deal with *Time*, *Fortune*, and other major magazines to send him galleys of major pieces on businessmen even if they weren't his clients. He would then, a day or two before the publications hit the stands, forward them to the subject of the piece with a note, "Thought you would like to see this. Ben." If he were abroad or the businessman were abroad, it was not beyond him to cable several thousand words of such an article to its subject. Was he implying that he had been responsible for the piece, or simply that he was so much on the "in" that he could get anything in advance? Both, according to some of his closest associates.

During my visit, I was, of course, suitably impressed with the grand entry and the grand mansion. Even Charles Revson, with his great, triplex Park Avenue apartment, which he had bought from the Helena Rubinstein estate, or Meshulam Riklis, with his magnificent Manhattan townhouse, or Sidney Weinberg, the senior partner of Goldman Sachs, with his august apartment at the Sherry-Netherland Hotel, hadn't impressed me as much. Revson and Riklis treated P.R. people as flunkies. As Leonard Horn, in weskit and cutaway, ushered me through the Sonnenberg house, what seemed most unusual to me were the high, ornate ceilings, the endless collection of brass, and the many rooms. All sorts of goodies, antiques, furniture, crystal, and art dazzled me as I passed, my head swiveling from left to right and back again. But no piece of art or artifact was quite as striking as the great man himself. When I got to the great library, there he was: pink under a wide, flowing mustache, wearing a purple smoking jacket and a red ascot, smoking a pipe with a wide, gleaming bowl. He arose with a warm smile and I was surprised at how tiny and frail he was, though he was only about sixty-eight at the time.

We conversed about people we both knew and he remarked how insecure many of the tycoons were and how their egos had to be constantly fed. He was surprisingly candid about lots of important businessmen, throwing names around without saying which were or were not his clients. But he clearly implied that many of them courted him. We were soon served tea, a giant cup for me and a glass for him, and he offered me tiny, delicious cakes. He complimented me on my work, especially because "you never forget the human element in your writing." It was a delightful hour, uplifting to my ego and impressive in terms of Sonnenberg's importance, affluence, and life style. Most of all, I remember the books. Almost everywhere in the library, in addition to on the crowded shelves, there were stacks of new books on tables, chairs, even neatly piled on the floor, as though waiting patiently for the host to get to them. Later, I learned, he read few books but had them read and summarized orally for him by a close associate.

"Keep up the fine work," said Sonnenberg as the butler ushered me out. "I'll be watching you perform with great pleasure. And you must come again for tea."

A few weeks later, I was there again, but as one of a dozen people. Sonnenberg moved affectionately from one to the other, introducing businessmen to writers, actors to producers, artists to dealers. I learned as time went on that he seemed to have either prescience or good intelligence sources about people. He knew when someone had the potential for advancement or recognition, and there was some feeling among those who knew him that once he had those vibes he used his influence to make the expectation come true. He told an executive of a large New York corporation who was in the process of building an imposing, new headquarters tower, "Watch that young man over there. He's a comer and you should get to know him." A few days later, Paul Goldberger, the young man he had pointed to, was named architecture critic of the *New York Times*.

"In the early years, Ben courted writers," recalls John Fones, one of his closest associates, "but when he became a famous personality, they courted him." Though he believed that the essence of a successful party or dinner depended much on the mix of people, Sonnenberg wasn't confident that those he entertained could keep themselves amused very long. He preferred to have no more than twenty at dinner. Hilda, his wife, was hostess, of course, but as the late Geoffrey Hellman, the *New Yorker* writer, commented, "That unpretentious lady with a useful sense of humor . . . has been known to duck her husband's parties and attend a movie with a friend." After dinner, it wasn't unusual for the twenty guests, as they finished with their brandy inhalers, to find themselves being joined by about thirty after-dinner guests. All would ascend in an elevator to the fifth-floor projection room to see an as yet unreleased film. It would be followed by a late-evening snack of roast beef sandwiches and highballs served by footmen in the candlelit, second-floor living room. What made the Sonnenberg home so noteworthy—besides its art, decor, and guest list—was its durability. While other great mansions were being shuttered, subdivided, or turned into institutions, museums, or galleries, it was still a private home. It has been claimed that more people were entertained at the Sonnenberg home than in any private mansion of its time.

When Sonnenberg dined out, alone or with a group, he also made it an occasion. At the 21 Club, which he particularly enjoyed, as many other businessmen did, he always had table 128, the first one at the right as the diners entered the main, second-floor dining room. Joan Crawford, the flamboyant movie actress, had the next table. Everyone would see first Ben and then Joan upon entering. If he had a 12:30 luncheon appointment, Sonnenberg would come in at 12:20, always early. He would stand in the lobby, staring with interest at the cigars and book displays, warmly greeting everyone he knew—and he seemed to know many. Soon, he would walk quickly up the stairs and plunk down at table 128, nodding to the maitre d' and the waiters. But he was never overly warm to those who serviced the 21 Club, or even to the owners.

"Ben was not the kind of guy you could kid, at least we couldn't," observed Pete Kriendler, who owns the famous restaurant along with Jerry Berns and Sheldon Kriendler. "He always kept his distance from us and our staff, although he was very warm to the important people he met at 21. We all loved the way he dressed, the dickey-bosom shirt and so on. But once when my brother Sheldon told him, 'You look like you just got out of Princeton, Mr. Sonnenberg,' Ben's eyes turned frosty. He didn't want us getting too friendly."

Alone or with guests, Sonnenberg always ate the same dishes. He had chicken broth with rice in a cup. But he insisted that the pot of soup be kept under fire at the table so that it would be hot when he wanted more. And he always had a grilled hamburger with a slice of onion—and kosher garlic pickles. For both Sonnenberg and Aristotle Onassis, the Greek shipping tycoon who married Jacqueline Kennedy, the Kriendlers and Berns kept a big jar of kosher garlic pickles in their larder.

Sonnenberg smoked his pipe intermittently as he ate. He was not a heavy drinker, preferring wine or an aperitif. And he rarely ate desserts. Even when he appeared for dinner after the theater, it would be for his usual fare, no dessert.

Tino Gavosto, maitre d' of 21's main dining room, always took Sonnenberg's reservations. "He was a marvelous man," Tino said. "We loved his peculiarities—and he was generous. He was not the sort of man you ever forget."

Sonnenberg, oddly enough, left an additional reason to be remembered at 21. Once, when a close friend in a moment of extreme affection seized each end of Ben's walrus mustache and yanked them in joy, Sonnenberg went into a tantrum. He rose furiously and raised his fist as if to bash it into his friend's face. It took Tino and a couple of waiters to quiet him down. Evidently, he didn't like being touched—especially on his mustache.

In his business dealings, Sonnenberg was shrewd, frank, demanding, and haughty with clients. To the twenty-five employees of his firm, Publicity Counselors, he gave a lot of autonomy, but he asked for superior performance by allowing wide responsibility only if it produced creative and practical results. Yet he kept his distance; his employees only spoke to him when his secretary summoned them. And with them he was alternately generous and sparing. Frank Saunders, now the public-relations vice-president of Philip Morris Inc., feels that he was underpaid in the ten years he worked for Sonnenberg. "But I'll always be grateful to him," says Saunders. "When I had a very serious health problem in my family followed by another, Ben deliberately piled on the work for me so that I had little time to worry about my family. I hated him for it at the time, but in retrospect he probably saved my sanity." As for his clients, Sonnenberg's demand that they pay no less than twenty-five thousand dollars a year and occasionally more than a hundred thousand dollars—a large fee in those days—was based not only on his appraisal of what he could do for them but on his way of life. He sensed that, once his clients observed his life style, they would feel that haggling over a fee would be both improper and embarrassing. He knew that he had built a personal edifice for his business career. "No question about it," he said. "I've become very adroit at this thing. I have a *couvert*. A fee of twenty-five or fifty thousand dollars for public relations is a drop in the bucket for a company that spends seven million dollars a year for the price of a double-spread in *Life!*" At the height of his career, and even when he gave up the firm to be a part-time publicity counselor, chiefs of top American corporations could brag that they were represented by Ben Sonnenberg, perhaps as they bragged that they had their own cigar cache at Dunhill's or their own measurements for custom suits filed at Tripler's or their own tables at the 21 Club.

Their demand for Sonnenberg's services and his demand to serve them his way were irresistible forces. But unlike many public-relations men or management consultants who allow themselves to become subservient to their clients, he always maintained the upper hand. It was perhaps one of his most intriguing characteristics in an age of proliferating yes-manism. His unusual manner of dress, his life style, his elaborate speech, his deep-set twinkling eyes, and, those who knew him best claim, his keen mind—all kept his clients in thrall. It didn't matter how powerful, aggressive or egotistical they were. By the time they had climbed to his library behind the august back of Leonard Horn to meet the great man, they were a little less than they had been when they had first tapped on the lion-headed knocker.

2

THE
PHENOMENON
OF A
YOUNG
IMMIGRANT

The short, plump, pink-faced boy of fourteen wanders, curiously troubled, but strangely excited, through the four floors of overflowing rooms in the Henry Street Settlement. It is the early teens of the still new twentieth century. The war brewing across the ocean has not yet drawn in the Americans. But there is already an ongoing class war, roiling in the urban cores, creating a seemingly insurmountable gap between the very rich and the very poor. Nowhere, perhaps, is it so noticeable as between the mansions at Gramercy Park and the teeming Lower East Side of Manhattan, only a few miles apart.

The boy responds to everything as he walks through the settlement house. Here the drama of old people, many of them barely hanging on to life, there the exhilaration of the young, there again the breathless aspect of a big-eyed, frightened young couple with the smell of steerage still about them. The ill, the well, the proud, and the uncertain mingle in a montage before him as he moves about, a stranger in bizarre surroundings, yet oddly drawn to them.

Skeptically, he admits that he likes the delight of the youngsters. But he also likes the dogmatic will to live of the oldsters. Somehow he can't help reacting to the pragmatism of the crafts lessons. His ears reverberate with the sounds of amateur thespians performing a play in a nearby room, shouting, declaiming what—Chekhov or Pushkin or Gogol? Drifting by another room, he briefly takes in the intensity of ballet dancers. Next door, he peers in to see forlorn men and women from sixty to eighty years old practicing ballroom dancing. It embarrasses him. Down in the basement, a lecture is under way in one section. A class of daubers in oils and sculptors is in another section. He learns later that a seventy-five-year-old woman has been chiseling a figure of Moses descending from Mount Sinai for almost half a decade. Upstairs, he is deeply moved as he makes way for a group of cripples who are laboriously crossing the lobby. Wherever there is a corner, an open place between groups, it seems, there is an old dodderer, a ragged white or black child, a homeless person, or a poorly dressed mother with a sniffling baby. All wait for some sort of help and soon get it from the staff of volunteers.

He stands off to a side, uncertainly, his heart pounding. This is the refuge in the ghetto he had heard about, observed from across the street, and finally ventured into. In his halting English, tinged with a heavy Russian accent, his few hesitant questions have only partially satisfied his curiosity. He returns the next day and the next and goes largely unnoticed amid the noise and traffic. But a woman with warm, glowing eyes singles him out and begins to follow him. It is Lillian Wald, the legendary founder of the famous settlement. She has seen his type before and she never ignores it.

Skillfully, tactfully, the tall, sensitive social worker approaches the boy and draws him out. Soon, he has forgotten his embarrassing accent, his feeling of strangeness. Why has he come in? He doesn't really know. He was attracted to the settlement by curiosity, as well as other reasons he cannot articulate.

Lillian Wald smiles with understanding and treats the boy to a soft drink. They sit in her tiny office and talk.

Was he, as seems obvious to her, born in Russia? Yes, in Brest-Litovsk. When did he come to the new country? Four years ago, in 1910, when he was nine years old. Is he an only child? No, he has two sisters, one older, one younger. What, by the way, is his name? He smiles a little shyly. Benjamin Sonnenberg. Where does he go to school? Public School No. 62, which is nearby. And so it all gradually comes out, prompted by another beverage and Lillian Wald's kindly interest.

His father, Harry Sonnenberg, has a clothing stand on Grand Street, where there are many such stands selling a variety of goods to people who come to shop locally and to others of greater means who come from a distance. Harry Sonnenberg left Russia in 1905 to make a better life for himself and his family in the United States. According to his son, Harry was hardly an overnight success, but he managed to hold on to his stand, acquire an apartment on Grand Street, and change his original name, Zonnenberg, to the more American-sounding Sonnenberg. Then, in 1910, he sent for his wife and children and the entire family was together again.

Wald senses some undeniable qualities in the boy, a deep strain of curiosity about people and institutions. She gathers this from his questions about the settlement, its origins, activities, participants. And she detects a hunger for articulation. His English is surprisingly good, but he is terribly shy about his accent. What shines through the language barrier, however, is an alertness and perception, held back, however, not only by an inadequate facility in language but also a lack of direction toward suitable activities. There is a quickness of gesture and expression in him that wants to break out.

"We have some things here," she tells him, "that you would enjoy doing."

"Yes?"

"Dance."

"Yes?"

"Dramatics."

"Yes?"

"Forensics."

His eyebrows have risen hopefully with each revelation but droop at the last. "Forensics?" he asks, doubtfully.

"Debating. People take a subject that not everyone agrees

with. Some take one side or opinion of the subject. Other people take another side. And you have a friendly argument about
it. Sometimes, we even have someone to act as a judge to de-
cide who is the winner. It's all how well you speak and how
you express your ideas."

He stares at her as though she has opened a window on a
world. His eyes glow. And now it is her interest that quick-
ens . . .

It would be difficult to exaggerate the influence Lillian
Wald and the Henry Street Settlement had on him. Eager but
confused, troubled by a language difficulty and by the poverty
that surrounded and weighed on him, the young Sonnenberg
probably found the humanity and the sensuousness of the
community house just what he needed to balance him. From
time to time, famous artists and performers would come to
Henry Street to mingle with the poor and the hopeful. Occasionally, the wealthy, drawn by curiosity or a desire to contribute funds, would appear to observe and meet the settlement people. For the next few years, Sonnenberg was to get
most of his recreation there, where he did indeed take part in
dramatics, dancing, and forensics.

He also developed the habit of walking whenever the
weather was suitable and when he had some time after school,
after helping his father at the stand, and later after working
summers as a stock boy at Gimbels. He would stand outside
Gramercy Park, study the locked gate of the private park, and
pass by the mansions and town houses that lined the enclave
virtually on all four sides, his curiosity aroused. Downtown
and uptown, there was a feast for the eyes and the senses. The
great museums of Fifth Avenue, Madison Avenue, and Central
Park; the Metropolitan Opera House; the art galleries of upper
Manhattan; the universities; Carnegie Hall and Mecca Temple—
these became the center of his focus. And the settlement house
remained the nucleus of that center. His senses were aflame
now and he could hardly understand or integrate the forces
that were transforming him. He was old-world clay being
shaped by new-world influences. It was a difficult, strange
metamorphosis, which was to take some odd turns.

Much later, he was to describe wryly this transformation

in the elaborate manner that was one of his personal idiosyncrasies.

"Here is the phenomenon of a young immigrant who, while he willy-nilly is dumped on the eastern seaboard of the United States, through a process of experiences becomes more American than Coca-Cola and assimilates himself to the point of knowing the latest boogie-woogie beat in the propaganda of his times. I could have sold rugs in Stamboul, but I became a ballyhoo artist. I was meant to operate from Bagdad to Trafalgar Square. I brought to America a kind of freshness but assimilated America's Coca-Cola idiom. It's as though a Paderewski became a Joe DiMaggio, or Rachmaninoff took to chewing gum on the stage and twirling a lasso, the way Will Rogers did."

In a sense, this comment, from Geoffrey Hellman's 1950 *New Yorker* article, indicates a clash of cultures. It is possible to conjecture that the young Sonnenberg felt the impact of new sensual experiences, emotional and cerebral stimuli on his as yet adolescent, naive personality. That is hardly unusual. Many a ghetto youth has had that experience if he has been fortunate enough to become exposed to the larger world around him. And most have benefited from the superimposing of one world on another. The question was, however, how they reacted to it—not immediately, but more importantly, at a later time.

The flamboyant intrigued him: the drama of art both European and American, the biting excitement of jazz and the power of the great classic composers, the beautiful styles of the fine English novelists and the pugnacious appeal of the journalist muckrakers. But how could he overlook the grinding realities that formed his everyday life? The tiny, crowded, firetrap apartment, his father's sometimes beaten look when he came home, his mother's concern about the family. Ida, his mother, prevailed on Lillian Wald to allow her to work as a cleaning woman at the settlement house. Ben didn't like it, but the iron-willed Ida insisted. She could earn some money and also keep an eye on him.

Ambition sprouted in him like a hungry seed. He decided to greatly improve his situation, provide well for his parents, and also seek a life that would be cultured, sophisticated, ar-

tistic and influential, one with perhaps a strong English flavor. He loved Dickens, Rudyard Kipling, Oscar Wilde, reading
at first haltingly and then avidly as his facility with the language grew. The English way of life, he decided, had a measured dignity, a disciplined enjoyment of bountiful things, an
unabashed sentiment, and a pervasive sense of good taste. Did
his perception of that life come from purely fictional sources?
Perhaps. But he was an adept learner about things that interested him. He read enormously in the public library, at the
same time studying people and how they behaved. But the
English novels he consumed contrasted with what he saw on
the sidewalks of New York. There was such a difference between the gracious cadence of English prose and wise-guy
American slang, between the rolling hills and mysterious
moors of the England he read about and the grimy canyons of
the Lower East Side that he walked through. Was he fanta-
sizing a more ideal life? At first it was all just an amorphous
yearning, but it was to take a clearer shape later, much later.

In the meantime, he attended DeWitt Clinton High School.
He was an energetic but often bemused student whose attention seemed to be on something outside. Harry never earned
more than twenty dollars a week, so Ben continued to work
during the summers to bolster the family's finances. It's likely,
though, that the work, as well as his activities at the Henry
Street Settlement, matured him early, providing discipline and
direction. All the while, Lillian Wald watched him, guiding
him in directions to which he seemed inclined. The short
young man, now speaking with an ease and style that delighted her, was slowly assuming a stature that even she, for
all her optimism, hadn't expected. It wasn't just a matter of
self-confidence, which he clearly had. There was another dimension to him, too. It was a puckishness, a hard-nosed independence minus any offensiveness. He was going to learn
all he could, experience fully everything that came along, but
he wasn't planning to take it all too seriously because he knew
what the real challenge was: to be what he wanted to be rather
than allow others to make him what they wanted him to be.
Studying him, Wald was both surprised and pleased.

One day in 1917, when he was sixteen, Wald left word for
him to come to her office. "You have grown up very quickly,
Ben," she told him.

He stared at her, nodding slowly.

"In fact, you've grown up so much," she said, "that I think we could use you on our staff as a leader. Would you be willing to take charge of our boys' club?"

He thought a moment. "I don't know," he said. "Do you think I can handle that much responsibility?"

She nodded. "Of course, you can, Ben. I've discussed it with the others on the staff. They fully agree with me. There would be a small salary and full board and lodging for you in the settlement house."

He could continue his schooling and live at the settlement, lightening his burden on the family's tight finances. "Thank you very much, Miss Wald," he said. "I think it's a great offer. I accept."

Two years later, while he still lived at the settlement house, Wald helped him to obtain a one-year scholarship to Columbia College. To raise money for lunches and textbooks, he became a campus correspondent, covering Columbia sports events for the *Brooklyn Eagle*. He liked it, but not enough, no more than his studies at Columbia. After his freshman year, he found a job at ten dollars a week plus commissions, by answering a *New York Times* advertisement that offered a selling job at the Chicago Portrait Company. So, at nineteen, he was a traveling salesman in the Midwest. He knocked on people's doors and tried to persuade them to have their old photographs tinted, enlarged, and framed, which he in turned mailed to the Chicago company.

Again, it was all too routine, too mundane for the energetic, ambitious young Sonnenberg. His real attention had been piqued by more creative, stirring pursuits than knocking on doors to hype a service to frowsy housewives. After two months of selling, he wound up in Bay City, Michigan. He had about forty dollars and a visceral gnawing to grab something more appealing, more exciting. He sent his Chicago employers his resignation and a final photograph to be worked on and then began hitchhiking to Flint. There, probably by dint of a selling ability he had quickly acquired, and claims of a familiarity with the New York movie and theatrical scene, he sold himself to the editor of the *Flint Journal* as a twenty-five-dollar-a-week reporter and movie critic. The new job was much more to his taste. But his short attention span with prosaic matters soon caused him to find Flint, an automobile-manufacturing center where the Buick Motor Company was the major producer, too provincial and uninteresting. He felt he was wasting himself and his still-burgeoning talents, and besides, he missed the pace, the exhilarating din, and the stimulation of New York. In the winter of 1921, he returned.

Now his life took a completely new turn, one that was to move him gradually toward the type of activity and life he craved. He went back to the settlement house, where Lillian Wald helped him once again. Through her influence, he became a staff worker for the Joint Distribution Committee, a charitable organization with strong American Jewish sponsorship, which subsidized war victims in Europe and the Near East. For the first time, he was exposed to big businessmen. One of his major responsibilities was to sell them tickets for fifty dollar-a-plate war-relief luncheons and dinners. But the postwar malaise and the difficult economy made the task a difficult one. Even Sonnenberg's youthful brashness didn't help much.

As the late Geoffrey T. Hellman related in his 1950 *New Yorker* article:

> He sometimes mentioned Felix M. Warburg's name, the chairman of the Distribution Committee, which he regarded as a talisman. Having beat his way into the office of Herbert N. Straus, one of the owners of Macy's, he urged Straus to buy tickets to a do-good banquet.
>
> The merchant hesitated. "Mr. Warburg sent me," said Sonnenberg. "I'm talking for Mr. Warburg."
>
> "What's the matter with Mr. Warburg?" asked Straus, an old friend of the banker. "Can't he come to see me himself?"
>
> Sonnenberg had never met Warburg, and he came away from this interview with a feeling that he could act with more authority if he had. He persuaded an associate to introduce him to Warburg at the charity headquarters. The Henry Street Settlement House had been heavily supported by Jacob H. Schiff, Warburg's father-in-law. Sonnenberg told Warburg what a splendid place it was, and the banker gave him a friendly

nod. Sonnenberg pursued his war-relief activities with renewed confidence.

And, to his satisfaction, he learned that most of the businessmen, bankers, and merchants seemed to like his youthful *chutzpah*. But he realized that that, too, could wear thin. He became an ardent tycoon watcher. And the more he saw of them, the more he observed their behavior and reactions, it's likely that it began to dawn on him that the only way he could really earn their respect was to rise to their level somehow, and even exceed it someday.

The next year, 1922, another opportunity arose. Lillian Wald received a call from Lewis L. Strauss. He was a former secretary to Herbert Hoover and a director of the American Relief Administration, a group formed by Hoover. Hoover, a mining expert and consulting engineer before he became president of the United States in 1928, had been in London representing San Francisco's Panama-Pacific Exposition when he was asked by the American ambassador to England to organize and direct the relief committee. Strauss asked Lillian Wald to recommend someone to conduct field work to help get food and medical assistance to the famine areas of Russia and Europe. Again, she thought of Sonnenberg.

Strauss hired the young man and Sonnenberg embarked on a whirlwind year of richly rewarding activity that was to move him a huge step closer to the life he would eventually assume. He spent six months in the Ukraine, where he observed firsthand the degradation of extreme poverty and enjoyed the gracious, well-served life of a humanitarian bringing succor to a foreign power. But it was the life of luxury that had a lasting influence on him.

In a villa outside Odessa, Sonnenberg and his associates were attended by a chef and five other servants. They were chauffeured to their duties in Cadillacs. He received a salary of two hundred dollars a month, plus a daily allowance of six dollars. Since almost all of his expenses were assumed by others, he saved several thousand dollars. And at the end of his mission, he went to Rome, then to Paris and to London. He apparently felt most at home in London, although Europe in general allowed him at last to fully savor the grand life. He stayed at the best hotels, bought books, attended the ballet and theater. "I had some suits made to order," he told Hellman, "and acquired a cane, a black homburg and a Burberry. The significance of having a man draw your bath and lay out your clothes burst upon me like a revelation. I realized for the first time what it was to be rich. I took a tintype in my mind of the way I wanted to be—a bon vivant, a patron of the arts, a man who could mix Picasso with Dun & Bradstreet."

In the winter of 1923, he was back in New York. His money was almost gone. But he still had his Bond Street collection of clothes. He got a room in Greenwich Village and tried his hand at publicity for fund drives involving Jewish charities and the Salvation Army. His role and his attainments, when measured against his now-expanded ambitions, were small. He tried writing, acting, and press-agenting for nightclubs and theaters. And then he took a giant step. For some six years, he had known Hilda Kaplan, a young, sweet-faced, but prim social worker at the Henry Street Settlement House. In 1924, they were married at City Hall.

But, even then, there was no time to waste or money to spend. He went back to his now feverish efforts to hustle a living and she returned to Henry Street. Later, he liked to tell his friends that their honeymoon was "a fifty-cent Chinese lunch and then we went back to work."

3

"THE ECONOMIC HEAT WAS ALWAYS ON ME"

There he was, short, brash, foisting an aggressive personality that was really soft at its core. He frequented Broadway, seeking doors that were ajar and could be pushed in. Hilda was working downtown, in and around the settlement house, being productive, earning a small salary. Ben, for his part, managed to get a few free-lance, press-agenting assignments for some of the lesser-known shows, night-club dancers, and a comic or two. Bravely, he began sporting his cane more, donning his homburg and his Burberry coat. It prompted some to think he might be British, others to wonder about him and remember him.

Later, they called it the Roaring Twenties. Then, it was more like the Hopeful Twenties. There was a feeling of undefined creativity in the air, an urgency to put the trauma of the war aside and make way for a new style of literature and art, new money, new ways of selling, and a pushy new advertising. Fresh faces were coming from the provinces to the city, beating the slicker at his own game. Materialism was acceptable, even desirable. Calvin Coolidge, Silent Cal, was in the White House, reducing income taxes and the national debt and ushering in a new era of industrial prosperity. Bruce Barton, chairman of the board of Batten, Barton, Durstine & Osborne, wrote *The Man Nobody Knows*, which presented Jesus Christ as a back slapper, a great salesman, a go-getter. A tin pan alley star, George Gershwin, shook the hallowed Aeolian Hall with his striking symphonic jazz composition the "Rhapsody in Blue." Paul Whiteman and his concert orchestra presented the raucous piece to great acclaim. John Held, Jr. created excitement and laughter, capturing a new type of demimonde in his flapper portraits. Having spurned the Pulitzer Prize for an earlier book, *Main Street*, Harry Sinclair Lewis, a tall, gawky Minnesotan, again won but refused to accept the award, this time for *Arrowsmith*, the best novel of 1925. Another writer from Minnesota, F. Scott Fitzgerald, presented his first novel, *This Side of Paradise*, and a short-story collection, *Flappers and Philosophers*, which seemed to capture the mood of the time.

In that heady, promising period, Ben Sonnenberg increased his circle of friends. There was something a bit quaint and yet appealing about this bright-eyed young dandy, which helped him be accepted by writers, artists, and critics. He was seen often with people like Konrad Bercovici, Floyd Dell, Harry Kemp, Rockwell Kent, Elinor Wylie, Louise Bryant, Harold Loeb, George Luks. Henry Seidel Canby invited him to tea. Sonnenberg tried writing for *Smart Set*, the fashionable magazine, but he was rejected.

Like the era itself, his experience in the mid-1920s became glamorized in retrospect. On the one hand, with about twenty New York newspapers, it wasn't hard to grab some space in a column, especially if you could place a celebrity of sorts in an interesting situation, time, or location; or a better-known celebrity within a reasonable distance of your not so well-known client. Innovation helped, but *chutzpah* was even more important. All in all, it was a grinding, uncertain existence, spotted with disappointments. The young, newly married publicist was always in financial difficulties.

In one breath, Sonnenberg would say later, "The next

couple of years was hard sledding but enjoyable." And in the next, "The economic heat was always on me."

He had to do something, not only to make a few more dollars but to satisfy the ambition that nagged at him. He knew that the brass ring was there, if he only could figure out how to grab it. And on a hot summer morning in 1926, he found it.

Dressed to the teeth, whirling his cane confidently, he entered the lobby of the new Fifth Avenue Hotel, one of Manhattan's gaudiest, as it prepared to open to the public. Oscar Wintrab, the manager, looked up from his desk to study the young man who came into his office. He blinked. The visitor wore a derby, striped ascot, a dark, four-button suit, and gray spats. His eyes shone with assurance and he smiled broadly under a flowing mustache.

"Mr. Wintrab? I'm Ben Sonnenberg."

"Yes?"

"I have come to help you make the Fifth Avenue Hotel the most famous hostelry in New York City."

"Yes? How?" Although a skeptical Viennese businessman, Wintrab was intrigued by the foppish but supremely confident Sonnenberg. "How, please?" Wintrab repeated, beginning to smile.

"Unless I am badly mistaken," Ben said, "you are going to have some fine jewels to flaunt in this hotel. And if we can make them truly shine, the public will flock to your door."

"Jewels? What jewels?"

"A figure of speech. I am referring to celebrities."

"Aah."

"If we can provide the right settings for them, the proper publicity and excitement, the celebrities who come to your hotel will draw other celebrities and lots of others who fawn on celebrities."

Wintrab responded by offering him a job, fifty dollars a week, an office, meals, and an expense account.

One of Sonnenberg's first subjects was Trader Horn, an aging, bearded hunter of the African jungles and veldts who was then enjoying the afterglow of writing a best-selling book. There was some doubt that the adventurer had actually authored the volume or experienced all the feats he claimed. But it was enough for the eager publicity man. Sonnenberg placed several newspaper stories informing the public that Trader Horn would soon make a public appearance. Convincing the Studebaker Motor Company that it would provide great publicity, Ben got an elaborate, open automobile from them, posted the adventurer on the back seat and proceeded up and down Fifth Avenue with his passenger waving at the crowd which had been alerted by the newspaper stories. At the beginning and end of the trip, of course, was the Fifth Avenue Hotel. Wintrab, who had never seen such excitement, was delighted.

Another hotel guest was soon singled out. Prince Georges Matchabelli had recently launched a cosmetics business after arriving in the new country from his native Georgian province in Russia. The prince was colorful and articulate. It wasn't difficult for Sonnenberg to attract lots of attention in the local papers for the gracious Russian emigre. Matchabelli became famous, almost overnight, when the stories and columns were syndicated across the country. Two years later, the prince hired Sonnenberg as his own press agent, paying him two hundred dollars a month to maintain the publicity barrage for his perfume company. Eventually, the fee was raised to one thousand dollars a month.

Meanwhile, at the Fifth Avenue Hotel, Sonnenberg kept pleasing Wintrab with his efforts. The Viennese had two other hotels, the Half Moon Hotel in Coney Island and the White Hotel on Lexington Avenue in Manhattan. He put Sonnenberg to work on both, and the results were productive as expected. It helped, too, that there was something European, continental, about the publicist, Wintrab decided, whether it was in manner, dress, or smoothness. Whatever it was, it didn't matter. The two men were meant for each other.

Wintrab introduced Sonnenberg to Joel Hillman, an entrepreneur who was about to open the George V Hotel in Paris. The publicist got a new account, his first in Europe.

So, in 1926, only a year after he had become a full-time publicity man at age twenty-five, he represented four hotels and a parfumier. Sonnenberg now showed the first signs of personal synergism, the capacity to blow a spark into a flame. Every time he dispatched a release on Prince Matchabelli, he made sure to refer to Bergdorf Goodman, a prime Matchabelli account. Through the prince, he had already met Edwin

Goodman, Bergdorf's founder. And when an article on the perfumier, containing a Bergdorf reference, was issued, Sonnenberg clipped it and forwarded it to Goodman. After two years of such efforts, the grateful, impressed Goodman gave Sonnenberg a contract for ten thousand dollars a year.

Sonnenberg had carefully built his contacts with entertainers, the more celebrated the better. He told them that the best place for them to stay whenever they were in Paris was the Hotel George V. He did the same for the Fifth Avenue Hotel. And rather offhandedly he told them that, if they liked to have a good meal in a homelike atmosphere fanned by cool, ocean breezes, they had only to mention his name at the Half Moon Hotel in Coney Island, where they would be warmly welcomed at no charge. And naturally he would parlay the appearance of any such well-known entertainers at any of his client hotels into publicity for that particular establishment.

Seeking greater exposure, Ely Culbertson, the bridge expert, sought out Sonnenberg. It was a difficult task. Bridge as a pastime was only then coming into its own and none of the newspapers was very excited about it. Least of all the *New York Times*. But by sheer persistence, Ben finally convinced the *Times* to at least take a look at the game in play. His particular target was a *Times* editor who up until then had stubbornly summed up his objections by stating, "We play poker here." But when Culbertson staged one of his contract bridge matches at the Waldorf-Astoria Hotel, the *Times* set up a telegraph line so that its man could report the competition rubber-by-rubber. It was a sweet triumph for Sonnenberg, and Culbertson was grateful.

Ben retired his father, Harry, in 1927 from the Grand Street clothing stand. That satisfying act may have been a watershed move on Sonnenberg's part. For the first time in his life, he could boast to himself that, by the actual and symbolic move of giving Harry security, Ben himself had arrived. He was relatively financially secure. His career was very difinitely on the rise, and although it was taking up many of the hours he should have been spending with Hilda, it was well worth it.

In the climb to success, he gave up something else, too, not often but occasionally: his pride, his self-respect. He told Julian Bach, the well-known New York literary agent, then a

young writer at *Life*, "I was so unbelievably brazen and cal-
culating that I couldn't help being aware that I was very un-
attractive to some people. [It went] from my meeting a blonde
in a beautiful fur coat when I made it a point to be seen with
her so that people would think I was her sugar daddy, to
courting Bobby Lehman at Lehman Brothers in the most demeaning way. You could literally say that 'Sonnenberg used
to pick up his sputum.' But, fortunately, I learned to become
more subtle, less openly brazen."

But something else had happened to him, something even
more important than becoming financially secure. All his life
he had been yearning for it, striving, pushing himself toward
it all those years when it had been only an amorphous desire,
a vague goal. Now he had achieved it. He had become an individual. He could not only create concepts around people and
institutions, but he could carry them out successfully. Moreover, he could do it in his own style. He tried to look older
than his clients so that they would be impressed by him and
listen to his advice. He had adopted an Edwardian style of
dress and he hoped that his clothes and the authoritative
mustache on his youthful face would give him a droll but reassuring panache. Judging by the reactions he obtained from
clients and the media, it was working.

It wasn't so difficult to manage. If you had an image of
yourself as you would like to be, it was easy enough to pick
up the details, the bits that you needed. He knew that he was
a quick study, that he had a talent for adopting appealing
things that others did. If you played that sort of game, it was
amazing what you could do. Once, he watched open-mouthed
as a dandy in a restaurant pulled out of a pocket a gossamer-
thin handkerchief a yard long to gently dry his lips. It was a
fine touch and Ben picked it up. Another time, as he bought a
newspaper from a stand, he saw a man hand the boy a five-
dollar bill for a paper and walk away without change. When
he asked if the man always did that, the boy replied, "Naw,
he only pays me once in two weeks 'cause he don't like to
carry money. But he sure makes it worthwhile." Ben picked
up that one, too. He began to rarely carry cash. He paid once
in a while—and rather lavishly. Bills were never handed to
him. They came in the mail. As a result, over the years he
became a product of the many traits he had observed and ap-

preciated. It was smart, too, if you had a clear concept of yourself, in his case, a gentleman of English lineage. Didn't actors, celebrities, and politicians do it? Who needed a voice coach or a grooming expert if you could pick it all up yourself? He could and he did.

In 1929, a year when he earned the impressive sum of twenty-five thousand dollars plus expenses, he rented his own office. As soon as he moved into the second floor of 247 Park Avenue, he hired a secretary and soon after a writer. Shortly afterward, as his business grew, he added free-lancers to assist him. Not that Sonnenberg didn't write some of his own publicity releases. He quickly learned, however, that he had to apply some pragmatic psychology. He would turn out different versions of each publicity release. The client would get one that was puffy and flattering. The media would get one that was shorter, punchier, and much more factual. Each served its own purpose and everyone was happy.

During the early 1930s, his earnings over expenses rose five thousand dollars annually. The depression caught up with him in a couple of those years because business was suffering badly and retrenching, and Sonnenberg had allowed his operating expenses to rise too much. But he had learned a lesson. In the mid-1930s, he decided to raise his fees, opting for fewer but better clients, especially bigger companies. Borrowing some money, he rented a larger office on the top floor of 247 Park. He kept his staff small, depending more on outside writers or specialists when he needed them. Some of his accounts didn't stay very long. Other relationships endured for years.

He kept his client list diverse. In the first half of the difficult 1930s, he had a full stable of rich clients. They included the Viking Press; Delman Shoes; Hygrade Food Products; Ely Culbertson; Paul Whiteman, the orchestra leader; the Book-of-the-Month Club; Russeks Fur Salons; Cavanagh Hats; I. Miller Shoes; Colette d'Arville, a singer; Elizabeth Arden; Helena Rubinstein; Charles V. Paterno, a real-estate operator; Bollinger Champagne; and William Bloom, an apparel manufacturer. He stimulated word-of-mouth recommendations. If he lost an account, he acted promptly to obtain a replacement. Sometimes the effort produced not one but two replacements.

During the second half of the 1930s, his business boomed and Sonnenberg changed with it. Gradually, his manner of speaking shifted subtly from the typical Broadway press agent's show-biz patois to a more formal speech and then again to his later grand, sometimes misty but Olympian style. "I am actually a builder of bridges into posterity," he said. He also declared, "I have always felt that in my business I am a lay psychoanalyst." The reaction was not the same for everyone. Some were put off; most were impressed. But he managed to express a sort of double message—that he was not only successful at his chosen pursuit of improving corporate and celebrity images, but that his superb personal taste gave him a substance that elevated him above that crass pursuit. During that period he could be very candid, backing up that implication of rising above it all. "I supply the Listerine to the commercial dandruff on the shoulders of corporations," he would say, smiling broadly. Later, he was to be even more brutally frank while carefully choosing those to whom he would deliver such confidences. His eyes had a way of twinkling at such times as if he dared the listener to scoff at his candidness or, for that matter, to fully appreciate it.

His profits from the business grew rapidly after that. His fees during the last years of the depression grew to two hundred fifty thousand dollars a year and during the 1940s and afterward never fell below five hundred thousand dollars. But increasingly, he put more of himself into his efforts to expand his business, going further than most publicists in this regard. His rapidly growing list of contacts helped him if his clients wanted a good seat at a Broadway show or to get ringside night-club seats, penthouse suites in the best hotels, box seats at the ball game, or reservations at 21 or another choice restaurant. Favors led to favors in Sonnenberg's world of Manhattan night life. Outwardly, Ben didn't mind being called at any time, the hour notwithstanding. If Hilda minded, she kept it to herself. And if inwardly he minded, he swallowed it graciously. Those days, he didn't mind knocking himself out for a client or would-be client. It wasn't time yet to relax. That would come later. Meanwhile, he had a pragmatic attitude: to succeed at whatever cost. To do so, besides extending himself, he sought out people who could help, and his manner, alternately winning and extending patronage, was just right. He stored up obligations not only to others, but from others.

Again, as his success grew, he changed. His growing stable of clients and the mounting number and diversity of his chores convinced him in the late 1930s that he should become more selective. Winnowing out his clientele, he decided that he could earn a great deal more representing fewer but bigger corporations—and especially their chiefs—than by promoting many smaller- or medium-sized clients. An entrepreneur and climber himself who apparently understood the corporate elite more than they realized, he discovered that exploiting this new pattern of more from less was a metier that he had been instinctively building toward for some time. Individuality was what he would give them so that each client would stand out from the corporate mob. To achieve that, he realized, he would have to exercise his own individuality as well—in his manner of work, the way he lived, and the way he conducted himself. He was poised for it, anyway, by nature and choice. He would be grandiose but somewhat mysterious, subservient to his clients' needs but superior to them personally. As to the media, he would curry their favor, but he would do it in his own style. He would appreciate them most in terms of cementing contact with their own elite, the owners and chief editors, or the best of their peer group. It would be more in a sense of recognition of and tribute to their accomplishments, public service, and obvious professionalism than for any publicity that they might render his clients. To do that he would handle the social invitations to the media stars himself, while his employees would make the publicity pitches. And, he knew that if he did it all well, clients would line up in front of his door and beg to be let in.

It was, he confided to his best friends, a sort of "grand scheme." And it really wasn't that difficult to set in motion, given the striking start that he had already made.

As early as 1933, he had tasted the power and money that came with serving several large companies. They did not mind paying good sums to publicize a new stock issue or the mounting of a proxy fight. Sonnenberg liked the bigger pool with the bigger fish and he decided that he needed some "touts," well-placed advertising executives or businessmen who would recommend him highly to others. Through one of them, he met the top brass of Beech Nut Foods and Squibb Manufacturing Company and he charmed them. The Texas Company, the big oil refiner, was another conquest at about the same time. It pleased Ben that he could not only serve them well but also mingle with their chiefs on a man-to-man basis. He began dropping most of his lesser clients, his clothing manufacturers, singers, and other similar types in favor of the big accounts. Through a stockbroker friend, Ben met Thomas A. Morgan, the head man at the Sperry Corporation, and he, too, became a client. The same middleman brought Sonnenberg to Juan Trippe, the president of Pan American Airways. Pan Am stayed with Sonnenberg for a decade.

And so it went, through the mid-1930s and into the early 1940s. Sonnenberg was now in the big time. As he put it later in recalling the shift in his business, "I left the minnow pond for waters where whales abounded. I now work only on a very high level. I am an economic snob."

And to carry that out, he created the proper environment and cultivated the proper behavior—as he saw it—to create the impression he wanted. He decorated his offices at 247 Park Avenue with wallpaper bearing Dickensian London scenes. Sonnenberg sat ensconced at the largest, most ornate desk many who came to visit had ever seen. He was driven to his office and his appointments in a large, black Packard by a chauffeur he had hired away from a funeral parlor. And he began acquiring a lavish, even fantastic wardrobe. At its height, its centerpiece was to be sixty-seven suits, all custom-made and all in dark shades with four-button, single-breasted jackets. Neckties? He was to have three hundred, at least.

Sonnenberg, in short, was on his way.

4

MY HOUSE, MY MANSION

Caught in a rainstorm one summer morning in 1931, Hilda Sonnenberg dashed under the overhang of a large house at 19 Gramercy Park South. Waiting, realizing that the rain would keep up, she turned to study the two, large, shuttered windows facing her. They were covered on the inside with brown paper, but by bending and twisting a bit, she could peer into the interior. Ordinarily, the clutter, the debris, and the spiraling networks of cobwebs she saw there would have made her grimace. Instead, she smiled. The house was apparently still uninhabited, probably still unrented, and hopefully still unsold.

Ben would be excited, she knew. Shortly after their marriage, they had rented a small apartment on Gramercy Park, a private park at the south end of Lexington Avenue between Twentieth and Twenty-first Streets. It was a cultural and historic enclave in Manhattan. Most of the four- and five-story houses ringing the park, but especially on the southeast quadrant, were the private residences of the wealthy. A few had been turned into a series of flats, and Ben had been able to get one. But in the five, grubby, striving, but exciting years since he had become a publicist and achieved some success, he talked more and more of owning their own home, one to make them proud. It might, he sometimes grandly said, even be a mansion. The august one, now fallen on hard times, in front of which Hilda stood, on the southeast corner of Twentieth Street and Irving Place, was just the kind of place he probably had in mind.

It wasn't hard to understand why the still imposing, five-story building was unoccupied, as were some others in the vicinity. Even the very rich had been hurt, some shattered, by the depression, scarcely more than a year and a half old. Although Hilda dealt directly with only the indigent—the poor families and the immigrants—and knew firsthand the dire effect of bad times on only those at the bottom rung of the ladder, she knew, too, what it had meant for those at the higher levels of society. She had read about it, and Ben had supplemented from personal knowledge what she already knew. In fact, as he had told her many times, his own success may have been due to the hardships the business community was experiencing. Hotels, stores, night clubs, many different types of businesses, entertainers, and even celebrities more than ever needed help in capturing the public's eye as they tried to stay afloat in these terrible times if not to just survive. His rising star amid disaster, he told her ruefully, was akin to that of doctors and, for that matter, of funeral directors. She didn't like that sort of talk, she had said, no matter what. His response, at least those times when they were alone in their apartment, was to draw her down to his lap, not an entirely easy matter, since she was somewhat larger than he was, and to kiss or squeeze her dismay away.

It seemed only a few months ago that Wall Street fever had gripped the country. On an average day, the stunning sum of five million shares of stock were bought, sold, bartered. No one could have known or suspected that an unprecedented crash was coming. Those who had the opportunity to know just went on making more and more money. On New Year's

Eve of 1928, ten months before the fateful October 29 of the next year, John Pierpont Morgan, Jr., had passed along "partner's row" in the House of Morgan and handed envelopes to each man. It was a bonus of not less than $1 million for each of them. With such a reward, they and many others had been lulled into false security. But so had millions of others, from the rich and the powerful to the schoolteacher, the factory worker, and the beggar. Three dark days had etched themselves on many brains. Thursday, October 24, 1929— 12,894,000 shares had changed hands, dropping some $3 billion in value into the void. Monday, October 28—9,212,000 shares had traded, the average price falling a record twenty-nine points, the total decline thus far about $14 billion. Tuesday, October 29—Black Tuesday—16,383,000 shares traded, the loss on the New York Stock Exchange alone being $10 billion or double the amount of money then in circulation throughout the country. Together, those three days had brought a devastating loss in the value of American stocks of $50 billion. It was half the total amount of the country's gross national product.

Hilda was certainly no stock-market expert. But the stunning numbers had been dinned into her by the newspapers and especially by Ben. He had spelled them out to her in other terms, not that she didn't herself possess sufficient imagination to understand the human dimensions of the calamity. About two million Americans were wiped out financially in the Wall Street debacle. Hundreds of thousands of homes were lost. Not only had hordes of investors bought stocks on margin but also homes, cars, furs, diamonds. Strangely, while there were some prominent suicides, like James J. Riordan, president of the New York County Trust Company, the suicide rate showed only a modest rise, which continued steadily for several years. But it was likely that many suicides were covered up by distraught, shamed families. Unemployment jumped as automobile plants slowed to a halt, in turn halting steel plants. Apple stands began appearing on corners. Families were torn apart as husbands lost jobs, trust between spouses failed, and children found themselves unable to understand why comfort had turned suddenly to poverty.

Ben had told Hilda about one of his clients. Sonnenberg had gone to keep an appointment with him at a midtown hotel. But when he arrived, he had found a crowd clustered outside. In its center lay the battered body of his client, spattered over the sidewalk from a six-floor jump out his hotel room. Ben had hardly been able to work that day.

Recalling those terrible things, Hilda found herself recoiling from them, trying to rid herself of their dark presence in her thoughts. But, she asked herself, was it the right time to move, to spend more on rent when the outlook was so dark? Wouldn't it be better to live conservatively, even though Ben was doing well, despite some occasional setbacks?

He didn't think so. And he gave her his own good, sound reasons why one had to seize opportunities when, and if they presented themselves.

Opportunity. Like a train that waits for you, chugging away, but not too long. What was it that George Bernard Shaw had said? "The people who get on in this world are the people who get up and look for the circumstances they want, and, if they can't find them, make them." And what did Shakespeare say? "There is a tide in the affairs of men, which, taken at the flood, leads on to fortune. Omitted, all the voyage of their life is bound in shallows and in miseries."

And then there was his own Sonnenberg philosophy. He was developing what he and some of his friends were calling "Sonnenbergisms," clever but daring expressions, which were self-indulgent, roundabout, and often contradictory. She couldn't remember them exactly but they sounded like this on his credo at age twenty-nine. ". . . People remain like children all their lives when it comes to impressions. The adolescence in that respect can last a man into his sixties, especially if he is of the self-made variety. The reason is that while he had the guts to carry him to where he finally got he always had to make allowances about what other people thought about everything under the sun. My relationships with such guys—and gals—is that they are more likely to be impressed about something when they see that some other guys or gals are impressed by it first. Now, that must seem like a paradox because the people who get up there quickly and stay there give off the emanation that they know more than anyone else. That simply is not true. So what I believe is that if I am going to get their credibility, I must establish the impression that I am a paragon in everything: intelligence, perspicacity, taste, culture and, perhaps above all, life style. If they see that I'm impressed with myself, it's as certain that they get their kicks from their achievements but their fears from insecurity that they will form their impressions about me directly from how I live and behave and talk and dress. Accordingly, I have to make sure that I impress others who will impress still others and so it will grow in an ever-expanding circle. The center of that circle should be, I think, a most impressive residence . . ."

Hilda shook her head. Imagine thinking like that when eight million people were out of work. The rain had stopped and it was time to go. With a last glance at the house at 19 Gramercy Park South, Hilda walked off.

A few months later in 1931, the Sonnenbergs moved into 19 Gramercy Park South. They took a duplex apartment on the first two floors. Hilda remembered for quite a while the look of pride, the excitement on Ben's face those first few months. There were several other tenants on the upper floors, but they didn't see much of them. Ben often told his wife that he wondered if the others who lived in the famous old building felt anything of the sense of the country's history that he did. Hilda had to smile. She agreed with Ben that the others probably didn't, but privately she must have admitted to herself that few people who had begun life in the United States as immigrants had Ben's hunger to live grandly. Some did, of course, but most wanted only to achieve a degree of financial security and comfort. Not that Ben wanted to forget his early years of poverty. He just wanted to surmount them. And to live in his own chosen style. She recalled with a renewed feeling of surprise the occasional times he had told her that when he had lived at the Henry Street Settlement House as an aide to Lillian Wald, his mother had scrubbed the floors there. There was always a pause in their conversation after that, and she sensed that even if perhaps he had exaggerated, he had felt a great debt of gratitude to his mother. And he told Hilda something else. One day when he had come into the settlement house with a bloody nose and a blackened eye, his mother had quickly put aside her brush and bucket and come to him. "What happened?" she had asked. "Some guys called me a dirty Jew," he said, "and we had a fight." She had stared in disbelief at him. Then, without warning, she reached over and thwacked him hard on his rear end. "You never fight over something like that, you hear me!" she shouted. "What do you care what bad people call you? You just walk away!" Ben had never forgotten it. Not, she realized, that wanting to live grandly represented an escape from discrimination and poverty, not directly anyway. One might even want to flaunt them. He took many occasions in later life to remind his family, friends, associates, and closer clients of his lowly beginnings. In fact, almost from the day they moved into their grand new quarters he had begun drinking tea out of a glass (rather than a cup) set in one of those metal holders used for glasses in which sundaes were served. It was a custom of the Jews of the Lower East Side, but it stayed with him all the rest of his life.

Ben soon augmented the research he had already accumulated on the history, the evolution of the house itself, as well as the park over which the imposing five-story structure seemed to be the stately guardian.

In a city wallowing in economic misery and human suffering, Gramercy Park was an oasis, a fenced enclave only for the wealthy and older residents who possessed keys to open the lock in its gate. It was still New York's only private park, almost a century after it had been laid out as a replica of an English square by Samuel Bulkley Ruggles. Ruggles, who lived from 1800 to 1881, was a successful New York City lawyer who gave up his law practice to devote himself to public affairs. He was an enthusiastic promoter of real estate development in the city, taking the lead in developing New York's water system, and was responsible for several private neighborhood parks. Gramercy Park was the only one of any size that remained.

The lush, green park quickly drew attention, and the lots facing it on all four sides were promptly bought by prominent New Yorkers. In 1837, William Samuel Johnson, a Whig politician and lawyer and the son and namesake of the president of Columbia College, bought the lot on the southeast corner facing the park at Irving Place and Twentieth Street. In 1845, he built on the north side of the plot a four-story house, a dignified brick structure in a modified Greek-Italian style. Strangely, for its imposing size and location, it had a simple front entrance so that one could enter directly from street level rather than step up onto a high stoop. That lack was later to lead to the addition of one of the house's more intriguing features—a high vestibule that would immediately impress visitors.

Some five years later, Johnson sold the house to Horace Brooks, a rich paper merchant who favored being driven around the city in a handsome carriage drawn by a pair of high-stepping horses. He built a stable on the southern portion of the plot that had been left open. A man with a zest for life, Brooks a decade or so later decided to add a fifth floor and characteristically chose a design in the French Second Empire style then much in vogue and topped it with a mansard border of black-painted cast iron. On the front, he added four bay windows separated by three high chimneys. The effect was to add an even more regal top to what was already a very imposing mansion.

After his death, Brooks's heirs sold the building in 1887 to Stuyvesant Fish, a descendant of a long mingling of famous blueblood families in the city. Fish was the son of Hamilton Fish, who had been a New York senator, governor, and secretary of state in two administrations headed by President Ulysses S. Grant. Stuyvesant Fish became a director of the Illinois Central Railroad and served as its president for twenty years, through 1907. Stuyvesant and his wife, the former Marian Graves Anthon, loved giving parties and 19 Gramercy Park South entered into its first long period as a center of social gatherings. The young society couple and their many friends enjoyed long afternoons and evenings in the fashionable house, accompanied by sumptuous food and entertainment. But the Stuyvesant Fishes wanted the house to bear more of their personal imprint. In the late 1880s, the couple spent more than $120,000 for some major exterior and interior changes. And to ensure that the then princely sum was properly spent, the Fishes engaged the most famous architectural firm in the country to design the alterations: McKim, Mead and White. Stanford White, the junior partner in the firm, took charge of the project. It was in part a labor of love for the dashing White, since he lived just across from Gramercy Park in a large mansion of his own on the corner of Twenty-first Street and Lexington Avenue, knew the neighborhood well, and had already redesigned several houses on the park. Later, he was to become even more famous when he was shot to death on the roof of Madison Square Garden by Harry K. Thaw over an alleged affair with Thaw's wife, Evelyn Nesbit Thaw.

In 1888, the same year he turned out the new designs for the Stuyvesant Fish house, Stanford White finished the alterations of the former Edwin Booth house at 16 Gramercy Park South, now The Players Club. The building still stands today, almost untouched, along with ten similarly large, striking houses on both the west and south sides of the park. The Fishes continued over the next decade to keep 19 Gramercy Park humming with well-attended soirees and dinners. Once in a while, they went overboard. Mrs. Fish gave a sitdown dinner for her dog and her friends' dogs, imploring the no-doubt surprised animals to partake from a heavily laden sideboard. But in 1899, Stuyvesant and Marian tired of the house. They prevailed on Stanford White again to design a new town house uptown on Seventy-eighth Street and Madison Avenue.

Despite the couple's desertion, they continued to own 19 Gramercy Park and rented it for ten years to various families of affluence and importance. Stuyvesant Fish passed on in 1923, but in 1909 the house had been leased to a builder who thereupon took the most strategic step of all. Razing the stable, he erected a six-floor studio apartment building in red brick on the plot. Then he cut through the south wall of the adjacent 19 Gramercy on several levels and transformed that structure, too, into a series of studio apartments. The combined edifice now had about thirty-five rooms and for the next three decades it was to be the home of many prominent New Yorkers and expatriates, including Ludwig Bemelmans, the writer; John Barrymore, the Shakespearean and Hollywood actor; and other celebrities.

Thus, by the time that Hilda Sonnenberg dashed under its overhang to escape the rain, it had bridged three American wars, seen New York emerge from a provincial Dutch-Whig-patrician city to the crossroads of the world, and despite the transformation from town mansion to apartment house it had remained itself, a towering sentinel of the city's only private park.

Approaching the house in the evening or sitting in his armchair in the newly painted, papered, and waxed apartment, Ben often found himself comforted those early months by that blanket of history and tradition. But it was all a stimulant, too. Only part of the house was his, and rented at that. He wanted somehow to feel that it was all his. Inevitably, this desire to occupy it all grew.

It wasn't that Sonnenberg was driven by greed. If it were that, there were plenty of foreclosed houses, defaulted apartments, and abandoned flats in the nearby streets that the owners were just panting to sell or lease. With his continuing flow of fees, he could conceivably become a landlord living off the distress of others. That was opportunity, too, wasn't it? Oh, no. His wanting to possess the entire house, even if he had to lease it all, was of a more subtle nature. It was its ambience, its close proximity to the leafy, refreshing replica of an English square. It was that aura that had brought him and Hilda, who wanted to satisfy his every whim, to the first, small apartment on Gramercy Park. Since he had first visited London and the English countryside when he had worked for the Joint Distribution Committee, he had come to love the English way of life. Particularly, he had come to admire England's Edwardian life style, when personal dignity, calm demeanor, and attention to propriety had been at their height. People cared about money and power, but manners, one's dress, choice of language, cuisine, and the enjoyment of culture were very important to them, too. That was the way Sonnenberg wanted to live. He meant to make it mean something for him, too, beyond itself. First he had to find the right stage, which he had in Gramercy Park. And then he had to find the right setting on that stage. Now it seemed that he had that in 19 Gramercy Park South.

There was another element, too, he told Hilda. He had chosen public relations as a profession, knowing that many looked down upon it. The patronizing attitude toward it was to a great extent justified. The typical Broadway press agent was a brassy guy in a loud suit badgering the media with a box of cigars in one hand and a whiskey bottle in the other. He promised the sky to his clients, sometimes grasped it, but mostly got a lot less. Business publicists, too, were also regarded in a demeaning light, because business in general, in those early depression years, was held in low repute. Sonnenberg didn't want to share in any of that low regard. He sensed that even a publicist could command respect if he respected himself. It harked back to his old theory that people aren't as impressed as when they see that others are impressed first. Moreover, if one could live in an impressive manner, even an imposing manner, one could give image making a new dimension of respect, importance, demand, even enviability. Sonnenberg realized that he was peculiarly suited to carrying it to such high levels. He had taste, discrimination, a deep feeling for art, and a talent for living in the grand style. If he could develop all that to an extreme, clients would want and need him and the press would be impressed—perhaps honored—to hear from him.

Consciously or unconsciously, he had already begun to travel that road. His elegant clothes, fastidious personal grooming, and walrus mustache had already made him the best-dressed and most distinctive publicist in New York. He was establishing an enviable record, too, with his placements and his professional style. Not that he was alone on that high level. There were also Ivy Lee, Edward Bernays, Carl Byoir, and John Hill, all skilled, much-respected publicists. Now, he told Hilda, he would propel it all forward to a much higher level. He would put money aside to lease a third, even a fourth, floor in the house so that eventually they would have it all, perhaps, as his business grew, even buy the entire structure and transform it into a mansion. Of course, that was years into the future, but it was a life goal that he was certain he could meet.

"I want my apartment and eventually 'my house' to exude three qualities that are indistinguishable from my person," he told some close friends in the 1930s. "They are credibility, stability and achievement. If that means that the neo-immigrant must become obsessed with people, position, patronage, and power, so be it. I am convinced that those are the levers that when pressed make the world go round. And I intend to press them to establish indisputably my credibility, stability, and achievement. When you hire Ben Sonnenberg, you aren't just hiring an expensive press agent and public relations man; you are also hiring a way of life that you might aspire to yourself."

It was lofty stuff, and very sanguine, considering the tough times they were living through, but they rented another floor, giving them not a duplex but a triplex. It was about that time, too, old friends recall, that another one of Ben's clients threw himself out of a high window to demonstrate his disdain for the world as it was. Once again, Ben was deeply distressed. No doubt, he felt that he had failed the man as he had the first man who had jumped. But, at the same time, he knew by then that some people do not want to be helped because that would denote weakness. A jump into the void, lasting only a few heart-beats, was an affirmation of faith, of will. He could understand but not condone. If only he could have reached that client more meaningfully. . . . Hilda, of course, tried to calm him. But she, too, felt the pang of a life thrown away. She dealt with it all day long in her work with the poor, the indigent, the street people, whose lives were an endless struggle that made one wonder out loud about the old homilies. *Was it true, Ben, that where there was a will there was a way? That the meek shall inherit the earth? That pride goeth before a fall? That sow and ye shall reap? That God must have loved the poor people because He made so many of them?*

Sometimes, they talked about it far into the night, frightened that he was leading them into a grandiose life style when chaos waited just outside their door as it did outside so many doors. Hilda acquiesced, but she was filled with trepidation. All his logic and rationale that she had considered only a few short months ago when she had waited out the rain remained, and she wasn't likely to forget it. But were they being unrealistic, too fanciful, too wasteful? That's what she said in those dark, middle hours of the morning when doubts most assailed her. Ben didn't say much when words weren't really necessary; he offered only an understanding silence. Clutching each other, lulled by the warmth of the other's body, they fell asleep and awoke some hours later refreshed, if not entirely relieved.

Often, Hilda felt that she had the proverbial tiger by the tail in Ben. His energy level, his restless imagination, and his immense drive sometimes frightened and worried her, yet they always amazed her. For a long time, she could not equate his grand ideas with the grime and poverty that surrounded the settlement house where she spent her days. But, in the final analysis, she understood him and his hungers. The question was, she told herself in the middle of the nights when he slept but she couldn't, whether he understood her. She was of a much calmer stripe and would happily have settled for less. At times, Ben seemed to treat her as though she were just a *hausfrau*, with limited interests and aspirations. Well, that was true, perhaps. But other times, when she suggested an idea for his business that he liked or a color, a particular wallpaper, or a certain blend of decor and background, his eyes would widen. He would touch his fingers to his lips and waft her a kiss. On her more sleepless nights, she would usually fall asleep with a sigh, half happy, half resigned. Maybe it was good that they were so different, she thought. That way, they could keep a check on each other.

And so Ben and Hilda gradually let each room subtly take on its shape and character, which in its outlines was anglophile but in its parts was a mixture of his—and her—own eclectic preferences. Ben loved brass. He had already accumulated a small collection, including some mortars and pestles, candlesticks, trays, and weights that he had brought back from London on his first visit there and added to. He had also bought a few modest oils and etchings. Hilda, for her part, favored heavy oak furniture, which by some odd coincidence seemed to go with the brass and the elaborate frames for the oil paintings that sometimes seemed to dwarf their subjects. She had a talent, probably related to her concern about their extravagance in dire times, for locating exceptionally good values in antique and rundown furniture stores. Ben made it a point to praise her when she made such an acquisition. He was beginning to get some clear visions of what the house could really be, really contain, and he was pleased, as any man would be, that his wife, though concerned about expenditures, did not stand in the way of his early efforts, groping though they were.

And, as its ambience developed more clearly in his head, he bought items to suit, which often by accident fell easily into place with those visions. And Hilda did, too. Glass blocks that Ben would use as ashtrays. An English bureau bookcase dating from the late eighteenth century. A hundred-year-old barometer. Ben also began collecting books—new, old, ancient. The heavy, polished furniture reflected the dull gleam of the books and the bright vibrations of the eclectic brass, silver, china, and glass. Somehow a very pleasant confusion rose from the artlessness of their growing collections. There was a burgeoning excitement to their surroundings and their friends mentioned it. The flush on the faces of the Sonnenbergs reflected their gratification.

By watching his expenses, by gradually increasing his fees, by putting money aside, Ben was able to acquire bit by bit more space in the building. In his off moments, he would increase his visits to the local galleries, antique shops, auction sales of estates, taking pains to make friends among the dealers and the auctioneers who might give him an advance tip on some valuable remnants that could be had for, if not a song, then not too steep a price.

By the mid-1930s, like his business, 19 Gramercy Park was beginning to show form, style, and real potential. He was making more friends and inviting more to his home. The word was beginning to get around: the Sonnenbergs knew how to live. Their social activities had a style and Ben was showing a real talent for making people pleased to come to his ever more beautiful apartment. More important, coming there seemed to leave a good aftertaste.

Something of a discrepancy remains among the recollections of those who attended those early cocktail parties and dinners and those who appeared there in later years. It involves Hilda. There is no doubt that Ben's reach to the social and professional heights was eased by an understanding, patient, even indulgent wife. Hilda personally bought many of the items that made the house so distinctive, helped by Ben's knowledge and taste. They didn't always agree, but the differences were amiable. His tastes were eclectic, hers more traditional and orderly. Ben liked to mix china and admitted that he wasn't sorry that the sets weren't complete enough for each meal. Those years, before she let Ben run to the extreme, she would have preferred fewer broken sets and less rattling of china as it was changed with every course. His taste, too, was for mixing the cuisine, along ethnic or national lines, while limiting the choice of wine. He had some eccentricities in his preferences. He would serve large bowls of soup—and plates of matzo. The pièce de résistance was a simple serving of chicken or steak (with no salad), followed by cheese and dessert. There would be nothing in sauce, dressing, or anything served in a casserole. He held out for simplicity within a stylish framework. She preferred a more traditional, although not necessarily a conventional meal. Being married to Ben must have been a trial at times, but Hilda is remembered as a gracious hostess, with a sense of humor.

In the later years, however, more than a few guests recall that she would disappear from the scene shortly after dinner. Although she didn't show it openly, they learned later from confidences Ben shared that the affairs had begun to bore her, especially when they became grander, the number of guests greater, and the conversation more varied and hectic. She would take in a late movie uptown with a friend or two or simply retire to read and relax in her bedroom.

Through the thirties and into the forties, however, she was a constant and vital part of Ben's social life. Their warm companionship was evident and touching. In fact, in a May 1946 column, "The Brighter Side," Damon Runyon, who vied with Walter Winchell for the position of Broadway's top columnist, wrote in the *Chicago Herald-American:*

> The little park with the iron gates to which only residents of Gramercy Park have keys, is just across the street [from the house]. It is a sedate old neighborhood and No. 19 is deemed a study in graceful and genteel architecture of its period.
>
> Benjamin Sonnenberg has lived there since 1930 with his wife, a most charming lady who was his boyhood sweetheart and who still sits in his lap in unabashed affection (a custom that I earnestly recommend to all wives), his daughter, 18, and now a student at Vassar, and his son, 10. . . .

The depression ended and there seemed to be no breathing room for the Sonnenbergs between that and the onset of war. Ben's business grew larger all the time, his clients more important, and his fees more substantial. He expanded into the entire house and then into the building next door, the former stable turned into a series of flats. In the meantime, he continued to expand his collection of art, brass, and silver. His close relationship with some clients was such that they felt awkward paying him in cash and preferred to reimburse him in valuable works of art.

In 1945, he purchased the two buildings for $89,000. It was a steal, easily worth double that price. But he had turned 19 Gramercy Park into such a personal statement and it had become "the Sonnenberg Mansion" to such an extent that the landlord must have been awed by Sonnenberg's offer.

Once he was the owner, Sonnenberg expanded on the changes he had already made. He hardly touched the exterior, but inside he transformed the six-story extension into guest bedrooms, studies, and servants' quarters. He added several more servants to make a total of seven, including one whose sole duty it was to keep the brass at a rich gloss. Gradually, as he concentrated on the showpiece, the old Fish house, he restored it to its former nineteenth-century brilliance. He went beyond Standford White's effort by removing the maze of small rooms on the top, or fifth, floor to create one of his more glamorous visions: a sumptuous, red-and-white confectionary ballroom with a professional projection booth built in one wall. When he finished, there were thirty-seven rooms in the twin complex—or three rooms each for the maximum of a dozen people who lived there. While the sum total was opulent in color and decor, the house had more of the flavor of a warm country home than the cold austerity of a city mansion. It was like Ben himself, sitting in the lushly paneled third-floor library and drinking hot tea in a tall glass. The heavy paneling, the square, open dimensions, the overall aspect of affluent ease without strain—and the unorthodox eclecticism—gave it all a lived-in feeling. Ben was very proud of what he had accomplished in the house and the use he had put it to. "Today, I can entertain as well in my house as in any restaurant," he told Geoffrey Hellman. "I like to get the illusion that my dining table has merely moved down thirty or forty blocks. My house, in a way, is simply an extension of the Perroquet Suite at the Waldorf."

Damon Runyon, however, wasn't about to let Sonnenberg get away with any pompous assertion about his own house. In that May 1946 *Chicago Herald-American* column, Runyon concluded his remarks with, "Benjamin Sonnenberg . . . is now of middle age, affable, companionable and has a great sense of humor. He takes pride in showing a visitor around his quite amazing house. Mrs. Sonnenberg has her sense of humor, too, because as I descended the last stair after a tour of what I am sure is the most spectacular establishment in all New York, I think I heard her whisper:

"The house that hot air built."

But Sonnenberg, in his turn, was not about to let Runyon get away with that. According to Jay Scott, a longtime Sonnenberg associate, the publicist had several hundred copies made of Runyon's otherwise highly flattering column, which he sent to all his clients and prospective clients—after clipping off the "hot air" ending.

5

THE
PEOPLE
ALCHEMIST

Consistent, that was the word for him. Even those he put off for the moment with a puckish, mischievous word or act had to admit it in retrospect. In the same manner that he first took two floors, adding rooms to his lease until he bought the entire house, Ben added to his clients and scope. First he added for quantity, then for quality, then for higher fees, and then for prestige. And, in that very same manner, he also cultivated people. He collected them, perhaps, as one might build a gallery of diverse portraits, some valuable for their intrinsic quality, others for their effect on the observer, and still others for their effect on the entire gallery. Underlying it all were two objectives, paradoxical in some ways but not to his view of how he wanted to command the life that he was building: the people he courted would help his work and at the same time develop his cultural and social perceptions. Others may have seen a conflict, a diffusion of objective in this. Ben didn't. Sonnenberg enjoyed it down to the toes of his long English hose.

He built his staff in the same way from the late 1940s through the 1950s. Slowly, carefully, he accumulated writers, media men, and—most strategically—an alter ego.

George Schreiber was a short, bespectacled, tousled man who had gone to law school but never practiced. He met Sonnenberg when they were boys on the Lower East Side. They saw in each other qualities that the other lacked. But, as they grew to know each other in a casual but budding friendship, they experienced the delight that comes not only from mutual understanding, but from a gratification in the insights that each had about things that they valued. It's likely, according to Sonnenberg associates who were there at the time, that he never made a formal offer to Schreiber to come to work for him. That probably would have been too direct, too condescending. All the staffers remember is that Schreiber showed up one day in Ben's cavernous, Dickensian offices at 247 Park Avenue, took up a corner spot in one section of the suite and became a fixture there as he did in Gramercy Park.

The handful of people who worked in the Sonnenberg office and his growing list of clients quickly learned to respect Schreiber. Educated at Harvard, self-effacing but possessed of a fabulous memory and facility, Schreiber helped Ben in two major ways. Since he read everything and could store it away or discard it depending upon how he evaluated its worth or pertinence, Schreiber slid into a role of alerting the publicist as to the thought trends that were stirring American society or Americans-at-large. He was Sonnenberg's intelligence man. Schreiber read all the New York newspapers, the *Washington Post*, the *Wall Street Journal*, the *Harvard Business Review*, several law journals, *Atlantic*, *Harper's*, the *Saturday Evening Post*, *Collier's*—and many books. He and Ben met at least once a day, usually more often. Carefully Ben listened, drinking his tea, as Schreiber delivered a monologue on ideas he had run across or trends he had divined. Then they would discuss them, Sonnenberg in turn storing away or discarding information, as he chose.

After a while, Schreiber found himself sliding into another role: that of chief counselor, amanuensis, alter ego. If, because of Schreiber, Ben seemed a little ahead of most people on what the main issues in American life were and who was on either side of them, it seemed natural to test other things on the brilliant and retentive mind of the nonpracticing lawyer. No one on the office staff or among the clients and their cohorts quite understood what Ben saw in this tousled guy who was such a quick read. But it soon became evident what George saw in Ben: stature, someone larger than life. Sonnenberg had the dash, personal presence, and ability to manipulate the world the way he liked. He also admired Ben's mind. All in all, what he saw in Ben pleased, excited, and gratified him, so much that he spent more than thirty happy years as his personal aide.

Along with Schreiber, there was Jeanette Blader, a determined, efficient secretary who, in her many years with Sonnenberg, learned to anticipate his needs and moods; and Charley Bick, who became Ben's accountant, tax adviser, financial controller, and arbiter of fees and contracts.

Schreiber, Blader, and Bick kept Sonnenberg insulated from the world of detail, dross, and mechanics that bored him. Jeanette rode herd on his day, Charley on his finances, and George on his mind—only, of course, as far as Ben would let them, and he let them do a good deal. Consciously or unconsciously, he was building a Byzantine miniature, a mosaic of different parts in which he was the glowing centerpiece. You couldn't see Sonnenberg, even if you worked for him, unless you made an appointment first with Jeanette. You didn't negotiate or discuss fees with Ben, but rather with Charley Bick. And, if you had an idea and you were smart in the bargain, you planted a seed with George and hoped that it would take root in Ben's head.

All of this, needless to say, left Sonnenberg free to pursue what he savored most: finding clients and working with them; building up and shaping his house; and accumulating a growing collection of art, brass, and sculpture. And to indulge what may well have been his chief avocation: collecting people. The line between business and friendship often became blurred. It didn't matter. There were those who excited his imagination, those who were so piquant that their lack of other qualities endeared them to him, and those whose budding talents spurred him to help them. But he could be ruthless in dropping old friends or acquaintances and latching onto new ones, although he made sure not to create any bitterness in the process.

"I like to change my bathwater of friends by ten percent a year," Sonnenberg said. But gradually he came to know everyone's weaknesses, no matter how lofty the subject. It made him cynical about grandiosity. "I am not awed by big shots," he told Geoffrey Hellman, "because I know that a man could be No. 1 on the Hooper-rating [which rated radio and television audiences] and still have all the insecurity and unsureness that is not resident in the heart of a bellboy who takes his girl to a ten-cent movie. I am a kind of worldly-wise gent." Increasingly, his contacts blossomed when he invited people to his home, where he could examine them more closely through the rosy filter of his candlelit background. "I know the alchemy of people," he said. "If I had Guy de Rothschild to dinner, I wouldn't try to find richer men for guests. I'd ask people richer than him in public displacement, in byline value. My idea of who to put up against Guy de Rothschild would be John Gunther or Edward R. Murrow," said Sonnenberg, as reported by Irwin Ross of *Fortune* magazine.

The incisive complexity of his mind and a pixyish self-interpretation of how he regarded people and how he chose to invite them to his home come through in Hellman's 1950 *New Yorker* article:

I work while I play and I play while I work. I feel that entertaining is helpful to my general reputation and I also enjoy it. I don't have to drink the wine—I just like to hear it gurgle. I like to mix people up. I think a really good dinner party should consist of an archbishop, an authoress, a lady of easy virtue, a tycoon and a Powers model. Actually, the people you ask at night need not have a virile daytime point of view. When you have as many celebrities among your friends as I have, it is important not to subject them to people who are rubbernecks, autograph hunters or inquisitive about the movie star's final scene in some eight-year-old picture, because to him it was only an assignment and he doesn't remember it and he didn't like the picture in the first place. There is a certain common language that famous people talk. There is a certain recognition that they afford one another. As a matter of fact, famous people are themselves careful where they go, because they know that their personality is often not as well expressed in private as it is when they have their makeup on and they are on location and the film is cut so that only the best frames are preserved. There is another thing that you find very often: There are some people who are really only meant to come to cocktail parties, and some people who are really only meant to come to dinner parties, and you have to exercise certain selective qualities as a host, because in my book it is as great a mistake to mix the wrong people as it is to mix the wrong drinks, and when I say you should not mix the wrong people, I don't mean that they have to be all of the same set—quite the contrary. I would like to say the following: If you are a host, remember that you don't have to gratuitously invite a couple of people who hate the living bloody guts of each other and after thirty years of friendship have finally parted company, and if you happen to know So-and So is suing So-and So, and that they were just in court this morning on account of something, you don't have to ask them. However, you don't always know. Here is the trick: The smaller the party, the more careful you have to be. If you have only six people at your dinner, you have to be more careful than if you have twenty-six, or two hundred and six. So I generally give large parties, where people who used to be married to each other can go to different floors.

Sonnenberg could be disconcerting. Just when people thought they understood him and could predict just how he would jump, he would jump in a different direction. But he was, in those halcyon years between 1945 and the early 1960s, learning, too, about himself and about people. People who worked for him, such as Jack Fones, Jay Scott, and Ray Josephs, regarded him as autocratic and elitist; but he could turn sentimental, and even magnanimous, and surprise them. There seemed to be two sides to him, both of them unfolding.

For example, at 247 Park Avenue, he would operate in a private suite of offices that bore his own opulent stamp and where he, Jeanette, George Schreiber, and Charley Bick held forth. It was executive country and no one, either staffers or clients, was permitted without appointment. Prints of Victorian England, books and mementos of Dickens, Thackeray, and Laurence Sterne's eras highlighted imposing rooms with heavy, dark paneling, big leather chairs, and red carpeting. The master himself sat at his massive desk, puffing away at one of his many English pipes, drinking his tea or speaking at length over the telephone. Clients were received there by appointment, and most thought that that was all there was to the Sonnenberg quarters.

Separated by a partition, however, was another section, which he referred to as "my boiler room." There, writers turned out a scad of publicity releases, financial statements, annual reports, brochures, and announcements of all sorts. In those plain working offices, the technicians labored away, seeing to the daily mechanics that Sonnenberg himself disdained, having been given leeway to use their own methods and copy style.

This practice might well have dismayed an important client, but it showed that the publicist could be consistent while being inconsistent. As Jack Fones recalled, he had just read to the retiring president of the Thomas J. Lipton Company a draft of a press release announcing a shift in the company's corporate command. The president blasted Fones because Jack, an old newsman, properly focused the release on the new appointee, not on the great record established by the man about to depart. When Fones retorted that the media would naturally be more interested in the new appointment, the hurt president said that he didn't care, he wanted the release done his way.

Fones, upset, went to Sonnenberg. After listening, Ben said, "Let's do it his way—and our way, too." So two releases went out. The release was revised to suit the outgoing president and read to him over the phone. The original release was then sent out to the newspapers.

In several interviews, Fones recalled how Sonnenberg, who could be all business, surprised him by his generosity and humaneness.

"We went down together to Dallas for the opening of the new offices of the D. D. Felman Oil and Gas Corporation, one of our newer clients," said Fones. "We were excited about it because Felman had wanted us to do something to give them a better image with Texans so that they wouldn't think that Felman was just another impersonal, greedy oil company. Ben had come up with an idea that he hoped would work and the Felman people agreed. He suggested that they send an art curator around the state and locate some of the most interesting native work being done by Texas painters. The best of it was bought and put together in a form of an art gallery and that was installed right in the Felman offices. Well, when we got down there, we found the offices full of people, critics, ranchers, businessmen, and newspaper people, all oohing and ahing over the paintings, prints, and so forth. Ben and I took a lot of congratulations that day."

The next day, Sonnenberg and Fones stayed over and walked around town. "When we came to the famous Neiman-Marcus store," Fones recalled, "Ben said, 'Ah, this is the store owned by my old friend Stanley Marcus. Let's go in and browse around.' At the jewelry counter, Ben stopped and said to me, 'Jack, I just want to buy a bauble for your wife. I've taken you away from her for a few days. Pick something nice now.' So I picked out a bracelet, which she still has and wears only on the best occasions. It was pretty, with a small pearl and ruby mounted on it. It's worth about twenty-five hundred dollars today."

That, he said, was Ben. But in the mid-1950s, Ben showed his hand again. "My kids brought home scarlet fever and the whole family caught it," said Fones. "We were quarantined in the house in Bedford Village for about ten days. I called Ben and said, 'I can't get out of here, Ben. I've got scarlet fever.'

"First, Ben said, 'Jack, how come at your age you are still getting children's diseases?' And then he said, 'Just take it easy and when you get over it and the quarantine is lifted, I want you and your wife to go away and do a little convalescing on me.' So we packed up and went to Bermuda when we got well and Ben paid the entire bill for a two-week stay. In subsequent years, Ben would foot the bill every year for a month in Montego Bay for Jane and me. He would say, 'Money is no object.' And so we would go down there and stay a month at a lovely hotel at the seaside of Montego Bay, Jamaica, and as directed send the bill to Ben."

But, if Sonnenberg was kind, even generous to his staff, he also made it plain that there was only one boss, one head man at Publicity Counselors Inc., as he called his agency. There were not even any close contenders. In fact, as interviews with old Sonnenberg associates showed, there was even confusion among them over who were the number-two and the number-three men in the agency. The concept of "pecking order" did not apply under Sonnenberg himself. Unlike today's public relations agencies, where titles such as president, executive vice-president, senior vice-president, and even the lowly vice-president are passed around like lollypops at the pediatrician's, Sonnenberg simply disdained giving any of his staffers, no matter how valuable, titles.

Jay Scott, who worked for Sonnenberg from 1947 through 1958, now in happy retirement, writes a Broadway chit-chat column for a New Jersey weekly, said that Sonnenberg was demanding of his people but didn't want to know the details of how they went about their work. Ben, eager to obtain major exposure of one of his choice clients, once said to Scott, "I don't want to know how you get the client on the cover of *Time*. I don't care what girl you have to sleep with to get it done. That's your business. Just get it done."

Ben's associates almost never, with the exception of Schreiber, participated in his social activities. But once Scott and the others were invited to a function at 19 Gramercy Park South where Theodore Kheel, the labor arbitrator, and a number of union officials were present. Scott remembers one of the union men kidding Sonnenberg, "Ben, you lived in Brooklyn, didn't you?" Sonnenberg replied, "You're not so far off. But if it weren't for you fellows, I could say that I came from some fancy place in Europe. You know me all too well."

Scott also recalls the unbelieving reaction of the union officials that evening when they found themselves waited on hand and foot by a haughty butler and waiters in cutaways and white gloves.

Although generally he kept his distance by staying in his office and out of "the boiler room," occasionally Sonnenberg would drift in and sit with one of the staffers. He would surprise them by reminiscing about his early days on the Lower East Side. For instance, he would retell the story of how his mother smacked him because he had fought after being called "a dirty Jew." Another time he recalled with misting eyes his mother had scrubbed the floors at the settlement house "for me." Another time, he told Scott, "I'm going to play gin rummy with my doctor this afternoon although I'm terribly busy. He deserves it because he delivered my children for free." Did Ben exaggerate the point for effect? "I don't know about that," Scott said. "It certainly made an effect on me. Ben was very credible."

Among Scott's other reminiscences was a different version of the well-known one involving Sonnenberg's help to Ely Culbertson, the bridge expert. According to Scott, the manager of the Fifth Avenue Hotel called in Sonnenberg, his press agent, and told him that a family living in the hotel owed it six hundred dollars and appeared unable to come up with the funds. "Go see the father," the manager said. "He's some kind of bridge expert or something. See if you can get him some exposure in the press so he can pay his bill." The man, of course, turned out to be Ely Culbertson, and Ben's successful effort to obtain some publicity for him proved to be significant for the man and his family.

Scott also recalls Sonnenberg visiting the *New York Times* often in the late 1940s and the 1950s to see editors and reporters, creating something of a stir in his homburg, chesterfield, and spats. He may have felt more at home there than at the tabloids and sensation-hungry papers.

John O'Hara, the short-story writer and novelist, was also a member of Sonnenberg's stable of writers. O'Hara seemed to have a special place in Ben's affection. One reason, Scott conjectures, is that the publicist on occasion had to tour the Manhattan bars, in his chauffeured limousine of course, to seek out O'Hara. It was one of those indulgences on his part that probably secretly pleased him. Talent, no doubt, he thought, had its own idiosyncrasies, and he really didn't mind chasing O'Hara, who seemed to move speedily, if shakily, from bar to bar.

Scott also remembers Sonnenberg giving an address at the New School, a liberal-arts college in Manhattan. Asked by a student how he had managed to get a *Time* cover article on Charles Luckman, the chairman of Lever Brothers, Ben replied, "First you get the account, the rest is simple. You get him on the cover of *Time* magazine."

with some of the many people Sonnenberg
ployed over the years in the pursuit of "the
ple" provide more than a few fascinating in-
im, which apparently have not been publicly

Matt, a vice-president and financial news director of Carl oir and Associates, recalls that Sonnenberg was
summoned in the late 1930s by the Texaco Company for an
unusual assignment. He was unprepared for the task, although he had been on retainer with Texaco for an earlier
assignment to help publicize their "clean, sanitary wash-
rooms." The new assignment was a sanitary effort but of a
totally different sort. Torkild Rieber, Texaco's chairman, had
suddenly found himself the subject of a muckraking article in
the *New York Herald Tribune*, which charged that he had been
a Nazi sympathizer in 1939–40. Texaco reacted with shock.
The war's wounds were still fresh in the public's conscious-
ness and the oil company feared a serious adverse effect, even
though it and its chairman vigorously denied the charges.

Sonnenberg had mixed feelings. But satisfied that the al-
legations were either unfounded at best or old hat at worst,
he rallied. In due course, he came up with a suggestion to
counter the shadows that had been raised, particularly in the
New York market where Texaco had its greatest fears of negative reaction.

"Why not sponsor radio broadcasts of the Metropolitan
Opera on Saturdays?" he said.

A positive reaction came quickly. It seemed the right thing
to do, and so it was, despite the fact that Rieber resigned soon
afterward. Texaco's sponsorship of the Met broadcasts became the single longest-running radio sponsorship in American broadcast history and still continues.

Matt also recalls that Sonnenberg served as an advisor to
Pan American Airways, later known as Pan Am, to keep the
peace between Juan Trippe, the chairman, and another, dis-
sident group. The publicist was similarly retained by the
Squibb Company, then known only as a maker of toothpaste
and cosmetics, to build their reputation as an ethical phar-
maceuticals manufacturer when they decided to enter that
field. It was a worthwhile effort, in retrospect, since Squibb
became an early producer of penicillin.

On a personal note, Matt, who worked for Sonnenberg from 1944 to 1947, recalls that the publicist, prior to retaining his own chauffeured limousine, liked to be seen arriving in a cab at the theater. But first he would take the subway to a few blocks away, hail a cab, and so arrive in style in his Edwardian garb.

During those middle years of his career, Sonnenberg worked hard on gaining contacts and influence in order to reach the power centers he needed for his business and life style. His early patron, Lewis Strauss, gave him an entré to the investment-banking house of Kuhn Loeb and also brought him to Robert Lehman, of the famous Lehman Brothers banking house. He and Lehman hit it off well, not only as professionals who respected each other in their respective fields, but also as men of the world who appreciated each other's instincts in life style and culture. They toured the art galleries together, Ben building the collection that he wanted for his house and Lehman accumulating oils that he would much later contribute to the world's most august museums. Sonnenberg also became close to Paul Mazur, a Lehman partner, who later assumed a role as an economic strategist to the country's top retailers.

Sonnenberg also managed to gain access to the White House, first through the efforts of George Schreiber, a Harvard Law School classmate of Benjamin Cohen and Thomas Corcoran, both presidential assistants. Later, Ben acquired additional contacts on 1600 Pennsylvania Avenue and Capitol Hill through Cohen and Corcoran. His Washington connections also enabled Sonnenberg to attract additional retainers, as did his growing Wall Street ties.

Both Leonard Matt and Jay Scott agree that Sonnenberg impressed them greatly, probably influenced their later careers in public relations, but withheld a certain portion of himself from them and his other employees. "I was confused about him, the real Ben Sonnenberg," Matt said. "But I thought he was brilliant and, well, a great actor."

In one of his most durable affiliations with anyone, Ben enjoyed a twenty-six-year relationship with James C. Bowling, the senior vice-president for communications at Philip Morris, Inc. It endured from 1952 until Sonnenberg's death in 1978. Their mutual appreciation was one of those unusual relationships that on the surface stemmed from totally different backgrounds, one involving an upbringing on big-city streets and the other a small-city, Kentucky environment. Beyond their business relationship was a chemical and cultural harmony that flowered over the years and brought each other considerable enjoyment, even understanding.

In interviews, Bowling spoke glowingly in his low-key way of his experiences with Sonnenberg: "I would go down to have lunch with him at Gramercy Park, once a month at least, for years, and sit first in his den and talk. And then have lunch in that delightful, little English room that he had down on the ground floor and talk for hours. We kept in touch all the time. He had so many relationships and I don't list myself among the most expert who knew him best but I would include myself among those who admired him most. He fascinated me, and, as I said to him, it took me about ten years to really understand him because Ben always talked in similes, analogies, and so on. He had a fascinating mind. He had a great grasp of the human psyche and a great feeling for what motivated the world, people, and politics.

"Did he dress in that Edwardian style to gain attention? No, I don't think so. I think that it became a style of his and he had really decided whom he wanted to be and how he wanted to live a long time ago. And I really think he was filling in the picture that he created himself. I believe he dressed that way because he had an affinity for London. His trips there were very important to him. It was all part of an almost English feel and look as well as the picture he had of a tintype which would have been the time when he dressed like someone might have in 1910. I don't think it was an affectation at all. It was just Ben. . . . Let me say something that will help to explain some aspects of it. Later, he had that antique car with an open front—probably a Rolls—and you always knew it was Ben's wherever you saw it. I guess that was a time when he was really—as he would have said—on the make, when he was beginning to become really established and getting clients and getting people to come to him for advice, so some of that was a sort of trick that people in country music use where they decorate themselves to call attention to themselves and that's what Ben did in those days.

"He had that car that represented a much earlier period

because it was consistent with the way he dressed, the way he lived, but it also meant that everyone who saw that car knew that it was Ben Sonnenberg's—and spread the word.

"Of course, he became a billboard for himself. People said who was that and his name was repeated here, there, presumably everywhere. The way he lived was why he did everything else, eventually to be the gentleman-of-leisure of the world, with his own salon. That, I suppose, was what it was all about, that was what he was working for, and his manor house on Gramercy Park was without doubt one of the most elegant still active in the world. It was a cherished invitation for people to come there. It meant a lot to Ben later when royalty wanted to come there and stay there. As he explained to me, 'Where do you stay when you are in Rome?' I said, 'At the Hassler.' He shook his head, saying, 'But do you know when you ask royalty where they stay? They say we stay with the Count So-and-So. You must remember, they don't spend any money. That's why they like to come here. It suits their style, they know they will be treated well. They don't have any money. So they don't stay at the Waldorf. They stay with me.'

"Back in the early 1950s, I guess, was the first time he asked me to come and see him in his office at 247 Park Avenue, a building that is, of course, now gone. His office was literally like walking into a museum. It was enormous. The desk was without question the biggest desk I have ever seen anywhere. It was quite ornate. He lived literally as if he were sitting in a museum with memorabilia all over the room. It was a fascination. I remarked how unusual it was and I asked him about it. He said that because the minute anyone walks into his office they know that he has more money than they do. So it put him in a bargaining position with his clients. It made him more substantive to his clients or his prospective clients.

"He was kind enough to invite my wife and me to many, many parties and events that he had at his home. To characterize the different types: I remember a member of the British nobility coming to this country to raise money for some Victorian restoration fund. For that, and other parties, Ben would always put together a fascinating mixture of people who made them quite memorable because they were so well structured. He used the house as a stage and everyone cherished being there. Everything was the best. They were literally museum pieces, not to mention the brass collection, the art, and everything else. He used the theater on the fifth floor for different things. He would throw a party there when we at Philip Morris would premiere a television show. Those were the early days of TV and companies owned shows and agencies and your ad agency actually produced the show for you. Like when we bought the 'I Love Lucy' show, Ben held a premiere for it in his theater with a dinner as he did for a number of other shows that we produced. It made them very special occasions. He wouldn't just invite the newspaper people but the TV people, too. The TV people knew it was different because it wasn't a rented theater with whiskey and peanuts but they were with other people who were not TV writers and it made the event more meaningful. That was staging.

"The number of people he invited varied. I've been there by myself all the way up to several hundred milling about the house with parties in virtually every room to small dinner parties of six. But when I say he ran a salon, he really did. It was almost clublike. He might have seen someone's writing, for example, and thought that there's a very bright up-and-coming young man whom I'd like to meet. And he would arrange to have you come over for lunch or cocktails or tea or dinner with someone that you would like to meet. He did things for people. He put people together. That was his ultimate art. But he prided himself that everyone benefited from it. It gave him pleasure. There was no monetary gain from it. A spinoff effect was that people knew something unusual, even important might come out of being invited to Ben's house. He could simply bring a bunch of people together or he could introduce someone quietly to the chairman of the XYZ Company whom they might want to acquire or whom XYZ might want to acquire or to be on the board of or whatever. And that's what he did."

6

"I
STAY HOME
ALONE
WITH
MY FAMILY"

Sonnenberg was in the beginning a devoted father and husband, a kisser, a hugger. He was meltingly soft toward the children when they were tiny, in the manner of most Jewish fathers, behaving almost as if he were grateful for them. At the same time he delighted in Hilda because she could bear such angels. When he first saw his pink, wrinkled daughter, Helen, in 1929, he said that he felt his life was complete. But when Ben, Jr., came along eight years later in 1937, he said that his life was "completer."

When he could, Sonnenberg would take his children for a walk through Gramercy Park. He would show them Edwin Booth's statue, let them run after the pigeons and throw nuts to the squirrels. Of course, in the house at 19 Gramercy each child had a separate room, spacious and lavish and well attended by the servants—a far cry, indeed, he realized, from his own childhood bedroom. Later, much later, it was to hurt him that Ben, Jr.—actually Ben convinced Hilda to name the boy Benjamin II, but as he grew up the son would have none of it—would throw up to him the fact that he had been born the son of a rich man.

Life was satisfying in those early, formative years of the family. The only problem was the increasing amount of time he was spending at his work, keeping clients happy and attracting new ones. Hilda was always understanding, knowing that he was building something for himself and his family, but at times she would question why he was going beyond what seemed to be required in his business. Sometimes he appeared to be enslaved to his clients. He would go out of his way not only to give them the media exposure they wanted or he thought they merited, but he also would be eager to satisfy their personal desires. He got into the habit, slid was more like it, of tipping the maitre d' or the headwaiter or the ticket broker or clerk heavily so that they would knock themselves out honoring his impromptu requests. Money talked, and Ben didn't mind spreading it around if it could come back to him in favors. Unlike the very rich, who aren't big tippers, Ben became a notable tipper.

It was symptomatic of his anxiety to please for Ben to take time away from his family, and there were occasions, as the children grew older, when Ben's giving so much of his time—and himself—to others hurt them.

But there were also times when he literally stole away from his increasingly hectic business life to stay with the family. Later, he would tell Geoffrey Hellman, "I stay home alone with my family two or three nights a week." But that, of course, left four or five other nights of the week when he didn't.

Sonnenberg gave Helen and Ben, Jr., everything they wanted, and more. They went to private schools, of course, and had summer vacations away even while their father stayed in the city to attend to his burgeoning business. Hilda would take over the combined role of mother-father at such times. Despite Hilda's efforts, Ben's increasing absences had a more harmful effect on his son than on his daughter.

Why was that? Obviously, those close to Sonnenberg say, it reflects the different reactions of daughters and sons toward their parents, especially their father. "Helen always seemed to love her father very much," observes Jack Fones. "Daughters can always understand better than sons why the father stays away because he's working hard. I guess sons need the companionship of a father to carry them through the difficult early years of adolescence and puberty. The fact is that Ben, Jr., showed the lack of it. He resented Ben's not being around enough. I suppose part of it, too, is the burden boys feel when they have a famous, successful father. There's a gap when the father doesn't pay them enough attention, complicated by the fact that kids like that feel they have to measure up to Dad."

The result was that the boy didn't have many friends and was lonely. And Ben's efforts to correct the situation had an opposite effect. Sonnenberg built a tiny gym in his basement for Ben, Jr.'s, use. But preadolescent boys need someone else with whom to play and enjoy physical activities, even if it's only tossing a ball around; so Sonnenberg would hire a local kid for twenty-five cents to come in and work out in the gym with Ben, Jr. It was obvious how futile this was. Few children would appreciate being paid to play in another kid's gym; rather, they would think the other kid was strange because he couldn't make friends on his own.

As for Hilda, in the early years she enjoyed the role of hostess and found herself excited, even inspired, by the glamor and repute of many of Ben's guests. The home was as much her's as Ben's, at least most of it; but gradually she lost her joy in the parties. There were too many, they came too often, and try as she might not to admit it, she felt left out of some of them. She realized that the guests came to see Ben and to meet the other guests. More and more, she thought she saw a patronizing gleam in their eyes when Ben introduced her. So this is Ben Sonnenberg's wife, they seemed to be thinking; she doesn't have his panache, flair, flavor. She's just a nice, friendly, average kind of housewife, in spite of the lush, sophisticated house and her famous husband. She also knew, perhaps with more certainty, that others who met her for the first time saw her differently. Her unassuming, cheerful personality, they were thinking, was just the right foil for Ben Sonnenberg and his increasingly flamboyant ways. Behind the reputed publicist was a quiet but well-balanced homemaker who kept him steady.

Although she was bothered by the condescension she saw

in the eyes of some of her husband's guests, she kept telling herself that she would not fall into the trap of believing that Ben was getting away from her, outgrowing her, beginning to occupy a different world. No, that would never happen. They cared for each other too much. Yet, as a sensible, realistic woman, she knew that it could happen, just as it had happened to many other couples.

Ben's activities expanded and Hilda's interest in the social aspect of his life faded, her prime interest became taking care of her children, her home, and Ben. She did not feel an equal obligation to be part of his social apparatus, along with the butler, the chef and the other servants. She persevered, but there were occasions when she simply disappeared. She may have been "an unpretentious lady with a useful sense of humor," as Hellman described her, but there were those times when it was simply better for her psyche, her nervous system, or merely her own sense of values to quietly leave the party and sit in the balcony of a Broadway show or in a neighborhood movie with a friend or neighbor.

A guest in the Sonnenberg home in the late 1940s still retains two vivid recollections.

During cocktails before dinner, a young man who was an undergraduate at Brown University came in to pick up Helen for their first date. As Helen introduced the boy to Hilda and Ben, and then to the sundry guests, all being attended by Leonard Horn and the other servants, the guest could see the young man swallow and look around with open mouth. It happened that particular evening that Ben's guests included some quite famous names. As the boy was paraded around to meet one after another, it was obvious that he felt overwhelmed. "Where could he take this girl who comes from such obvious wealth and opulence?" the guest wondered. "How many young men find themselves calling on a girl in a mansion with only candlelight, burnished brass, and a lot of celebrities?" He concluded that the situation, which must have been repeated at least several times with other young men, must have proved a problem for Ben's daughter.

The other recollection involved Ben, Jr. After the diners on another night took the elevator to the fifth floor to watch the movie preview, the same guest was impressed by the sumptuous room all in red—red furniture, red carpets. But when he walked in, he saw awaiting them all a small, plump boy all dressed up in a suit sitting in one of the red armchairs. Obviously, he, too, was waiting for the movie. What, pondered the guest, was the child doing up so late, all dressed up for the movie? "Why isn't he doing his homework or, better still, sleeping so he can get to school in the morning?"

Ben, Jr., in fact, it became painfully aware over the years, was the least of the family members to feel at home at 19 Gramercy Park South. The thirty-seven-room mansion was never big enough for him. It wasn't a question of size as much as spirit, style, environment. He used to tell friends, when he would meet them at one or another of the New York museums, that he felt more at home there. Why? Because the armed guards were more friendly to him, more polite, than the servants in his own home. "At home, by contrast," he wrote many years later in an article for *The Nation*, "I was a kid at the mercy of angry help."

At its peak, the staff numbered thirteen members, some of whom treated the boy as a pest. It may have been more than that, too, based on his own elaboration of that treatment in the article.

Then the house was ruled more with reference to the wishes and expectations of its large, exceedingly specialized staff than with thought (as I thought) of my own childish good. I had status, the servants had power. We had fights and they always won. *Real* English butlers and *real* Irish maids, they afflicted me with the moral zeal of the disciplined but disenfranchised, avid to show where I had failed. With what literal force I later read, *And I have seen the eternal Footman hold my coat, and snicker.* I acted toward them vengefully, in turn, consoling myself by reflecting upon their replaceability. That was the ultimate fact, was it not? A wretched result has been that I still think status of more worth than power.

And yet how replaceable were they? The English butlers, one formerly with HRH the Duke of Windsor, another with Myron T. Herrick, our ambassador to France: a butler who, moreover, on May 21, 1927, loaned Lindbergh a pair of pajamas? The servants were truly needed. It showed in the numerous valuable plates they presented at even family meals, ceremonially, not to be eaten from; in the deference of silence to which they appeared, and which to me from an early age made a paradox of the then common ideal of unobtrusive service; and in their great importance as topics of conversation. They were needed besides as mirrors, implicated thereby in the buying of very vast numbers of shoes and clothes which it also was their job to care for. . . .

Young Sonnenberg also had some problems with a German governess during World War II who fully expected the Nazis to take over New York. "She was openly pro-German after the Allied bombing of Metz in her home region of Moselle," he wrote. "In fact, she went off her head. She started telling me what I could do when the Nazis took over New York. 'Just don't mention you're Jewish.'"

I was Jewish? I knew and I didn't know. It wasn't exactly a secret. My parents spoke Yiddish fluently; my grandparents lived on the Lower East Side; Bernard Baruch, Albert Einstein, Leslie Howard made us proud. Yet to look at the walls with their portraits of Millicent, Duchess of Sutherland, of Lady Ottoline Morrell, at the Queen Anne this and the Charles the First that, at the bust of Pope and the braces that had once belonged to Disraeli—surely I wasn't Jewish? Or if I were, then so what? To ask, as it were of the Duchess or of my father's still more ducal "man," was to invite the answer. *You are as Jewish as you want to be.* That was the answer I got. Little wonder that then it was left to one in a lunacy of sorrow to bring the effect of my question well and truly home.

In some ways, he was a difficult young man, rebelling at times against his parents, scoffing at their life style, their emphasis on objects and the grand way of life. He relates in his articles that he had "an actual physical fight" with a butler who had been instructed not to let him go out of the house.

And some years later "I stole expensive objets d'art to give to my girlfriend. . . ."

His growing-up difficulties were understandable. If Ben, Sr., had been born "an old man," Ben, Jr., matured slowly because of it. Although the father loved the son, not only said so but showed it in many ways by indulging the boy, the lack of real communication between them grew. The father had pulled himself up by the bootstraps and the cliché implicit in that was real and justifiable to Ben, Sr., because everything he had done came down to an effort to "get out of the Lower East Side forever." Ben, Jr., had been born at 19 Gramercy Park, born into that better life. Taking it all for granted, he didn't have to appreciate it. It was there and he could criticize its dross elements. It's likely, too, that the more successful the father became, the less he could talk to the son and earn his understanding or respect.

"All our cars were outlandish-looking custom-built affairs," the son wrote, "more stately comfortable carriage than streamlined automobile, nothing racy or aerodynamic like Ellery Queen's Duesenberg. They weren't machines but sumptuous small interiors that moved, implying a not truly high regard for travel, let along speed. 'Brewster body on a '39 Ford chassis.' That sort of car. The chauffeur was always having to say; otherwise no one could know. 'A '41 Packard town car,' noticeable on the rainiest night outside of '21.' Each of our cars had a pedigree, too. Somebody prominent had had it built. This or that 'Mrs. Warren Wampum, a name as old as the Hudson.' None was new with us."

On Sundays, Ben Jr., recalled, they were driven in one of the cars to his grandmother's for lunch on Riverside Drive. In the spring and summers, a prewar Cadillac took them to a summer house. "We rented from people who'd never seen Jews up close before. My mother and father liked making this point. Their own kind could no longer rent as we could, bringing a full staff. Mannerly bankers with soft-spoken wives, good-looking dogs and Purdey guns, they had been ruined in the '29 crash. Ruined? They looked sounder than us. Their state of being before must have been unimaginably intact. We always left them our new croquet set (we brought a new one each May). Why this exactly, I never found out. . . ."

Some of the father's friends thought that the son was very spoiled. One friend, who asked not to be quoted by name, said that "young Ben at school was very arrogant. He went to Lawrenceville, and Ben was very proud that his son was going to an Eastern prep school. Well, he didn't last there very long because he was just too arrogant."

Some years later, recalling a particular incident, the friend was coming in on a Sunday evening to see Ben, Sr., and he met Ben, Jr., going out. The young man by then had lived in London and in Spain for a couple of years and had run up some bills beyond his allowance. As the friend entered the library, he found Ben, Sr., sitting there, toying with his pipe— "he had at least eighty-five pipes"—and Ben said, "How are you, young man?" But he seemed "sort of a little abstracted," and then he chuckled, almost to himself.

"What's funny, Ben?" the friend asked.

"Well, I've just had a little set-to with my son."

Ben chuckled again. "He's a rascal."

"He is?"

"You know what that young man said to me?"

"What?"

"I was telling him that he was spending too much money, and when was he going to do something and settle down. I said to him listen—and then I gestured all around the library, the furniture and the furnishings, the grandeur of the whole thing—and I told him, 'Look, you know, you don't start here.' "

Ben now almost dissolved in laughter, adding, "You know what he said to me? He said, 'I did.' "

If the son was pulling away, there were also signs that Hilda was becoming fatigued or bored, or both, by her husband's evening activities. Those invited to the cocktail parties, dinners, and movie previews might have wondered, without asking, where Mrs. Sonnenberg was. But familiarity erased the barriers. Those who came there repeatedly did occasionally ask, for instance, "Where does Mrs. Sonnenberg go in the winter?"

"Go in the winter?" Ben or his very closest friends would reply. "She is upstairs in her bedroom."

"I see."

"Having dinner served there."

"I see."

"She's a bit tired tonight," would be the host's or friend's next comment, or "she's sort of under the weather today." Or, "She's resting for the evening. I think she's entitled, right, don't you think?"

"Right, of course."

Who, after all, could keep up with Sonnenberg, even on those nights when he stayed at home with his family?

BOOK
TWO

7

TRIUMPHS
INTO
SAGAS

By the early- and mid-fifties, Sonnenberg had removed all of the telltale traces of his Lower East Side upbringing—except for his stubborn trait of drinking a hot glass of tea at 4:00 P.M. every day—and had begun to attain peak form. Everything seemed to be working for him: his sharpening perception of how to obtain more and better media exposure; his ever-growing reputation as one of New York's busiest social hosts, his sensitivity about what made people tick; his increasing appeal to a growing number of the nation's business chiefs, as well as to some politicians and entertainment celebrities. But, perhaps above all, there had been some remarkable achievements, which brought many important people to his office and his home to meet him, listen, and then tell him what they needed of him.

Several of those feats, in fact, were becoming classic, contemporary sagas on how to make it in America and, more important, how to let everyone know about it.

During the late twenties, Ben Sonnenberg had met Henry Rudkin, a Wall Street stockbroker, and his wife, Margaret, who lived on a small farm near Norwalk, Connecticut. The couple had three sons, one of whom suffered from asthma. The boy, Mark, evidently had attacks after eating certain foods. Bread, in particular, seemed to set off an attack. Doctors advised Margaret that the boy, their youngest, would have to be sent to Arizona or be fed rich, home-baked bread. She began searching for recipes, testing some she found in an old cookbook, using her own instincts and trying to recall how her Irish grandmother had baked bread. At the same time, she tried to bear in mind the doctor's instructions about ingredients. After a number of abortive attempts, she finally produced a bread that she hoped would do. It included fresh, stone-ground wheat flour, unsulphured molasses, honey, fresh butter, and whole milk.

The first loaf was, sadly, as heavy as a rock. She experimented with her formula, varying the ratio of ingredients, and the bread was finally ready. She offered it to her family, holding her breath after nine-year-old Mark ate it. Everyone liked its taste and texture, even Mark, and she baked more loaves. A few weeks later, when she took the boy to the allergist, the doctor examined Mark and told his mother, "I honestly think he's better. Let me try that great bread of yours on a few of my other asthmatics."

She also served the bread to some neighbors. The reaction was similar, and they urged her to sell some loaves to the local grocer. The Rudkins had a family consultation. It was 1930, in the trough of the depression, and they were in sharply reduced circumstances. Like thousands of other brokers, Henry Rudkin had found his income cut to a fraction of its former size. They had pared down the operating costs of the farm to a minimum. Henry had also raised some polo ponies nearby, but the bad times had forced him to sell them or give them away. And so, with Margaret insisting, the rest of the family agreed that the grocer be tried. She baked eight loaves and took them in a wicker basket to the store.

Late that day after the first, hesitant delivery, the grocer was on the phone. "Margaret!" he said excitedly. "We need another dozen loaves! They've just walked out of the store!"

She baked more and then more again. But her old relic of a stove proved inadequate to the task, burning its contents and emitting clouds of smoke that filled the house. After a brief chat, Margaret and Henry decided to phone an old friend for help.

They told Ben Sonnenberg the entire story, and then Margaret said, "Will you lend us three hundred dollars for a new stove?"

He thought for a few seconds. Was the story apochryphal? It certainly sounded like it. But the Rudkins were decent, honest people. "Of course, my dear Margaret," he replied.

"Thank you, Ben."

"Please don't mention it."

She hesitated, then said, "Henry and I have talked it over. We are going to start a little baking company of our own. And because we knew you would come to our help, we are going to give you a one-third interest."

"That's very kind of you and Henry. What are you going to name the company?"

"After our farm. Pepperidge Farm."

After the new stove was installed, she produced a hundred loaves a week with the aid of a neighbor. Margaret found a retailer in New York City, Charles & Company, which ordered twenty-four loaves a day. Henry, who still worked at a brokerage in Manhattan, obligingly took them in a box to the city on the 7:38 broker's special every morning. A Red Cap would meet him at Grand Central Station to take the bread, dispatch it to the bakers, and Henry would continue by subway to Wall Street.

As the company grew over the next two decades, adding a variety of bread, rolls, and cake, its sales and output grew tremendously. Business went from twenty dollars a week to over $50 million a year, while production rose from one hundred loaves a week to four thousand and eventually to one million. Sonnenberg served for years as the company's public-relations consultant and was able to get Pepperidge Farm and the Rudkins glowing stories in *Reader's Digest*, *Ladies' Home Journal*, *McCall's*, and other big-circulation magazines. The

Rudkins didn't advertise during all those years. But word-of-mouth recommendations and Sonnenberg's media exposure helped the company's baked products to achieve an enormous success. In 1958, Pepperidge Farm was sold to the Campbell Soup Company for $28 million. And Sonnenberg got one-third of it in cash and Campbell Soup stock.

Then there was the time in the early 1950s when the old Pressed Steel Car Company badly needed a new image. The Manhattan-based company, founded by the legendary Diamond Jim Brady in 1899, had for most of its history produced freight cars and later heavy presses and pressed steel. But since World War II, the company had diversified into a general line of industrial goods, building and consumer products, and services. It had even plunged into such glamorous fields as women's fashions. Much of the pushing and shoving into new ventures had come from acquisitions. In the process, management, headed by John I. Snider, had changed the corporate name to U.S. Industries. But it was only a cosmetic change, hardly warming observers and critics, who regarded U.S.I. as a sort of business grab bag gathered around Diamond Jim's old heavy manufacturing business. It was also evident from the minimal interest in U.S.I. stock by Wall Street and the large, institutional investors that something more, something charismatic or exciting, was needed to impart strength and character to the outside perception of the company.

Hired for the image-building campaign by Snider, Sonnenberg decided for starters to arrange a dinner at 19 Gramercy Park in which he would unveil the U.S.I. chief to a group of important editors. It proved a success, as Sonnenberg expected it would be from his experience presenting other formerly shy corporation heads.

Introducing an important businessman against a backdrop of an elegant drawing room to six or a dozen editorial peers served the best in food and drink by white-gloved waiters in cutaways had to pay off handsomely. Even the toughest-skinned editors succumbed, somehow walking away with the conviction that Snider was a paragon of the American business statesman. U.S.I. climbed a series of notches in journalistic estimation, and Sonnenberg continued to massage Snider's image. So well was Snider regarded in the next few years as a major spokesman for industrial responsibility, particularly toward workers being displaced by spreading mation, that he was even invited to address the AFL-CIO.

But both the publicist and the U.S.I. chairman knew that it was still not enough to make the company an attractive investment for Wall Street. An extra dimension, one that would inspire long-term interest and confidence, was needed.

"What do you think we should do?" Snider asked Ben.

"Your board—that's where the opportunity is."

"What do you mean?"

"There is nothing like the quality and character of a board of directors to establish credibility," Sonnenberg said.

"So—?"

"Why don't you change most of your directors with well-known figures?"

"Like whom?"

Without pausing for breath, Ben rattled off a dozen names of some of the most prominent businessmen, former high government officials and politicians, and leading attorneys in the country.

"Can we get them?" Snider said.

His eyes twinkling, Ben told him, "I guarantee it. Enough of them to make a vast difference. Enough heads of big, big companies or ex-congressmen or senators. Yes, John, I can get them for you. We can make it one of the most exciting boards in history."

Snider, a cautious but pragmatic man, nodded soberly. But it was evident that he still had some doubts. "How should we treat it," he said, "so as to get maximum value from it?"

Sonnenberg pondered the question, sipping his tea. After a few moments, he said, "We'll call it 'Our Billion-Dollar Board.'"

The plan was put into effect—first the appointments, then the announcements. This was followed by a bold series of advertisements proclaiming the advent of "Our Billion-Dollar Board" in major consumer newspapers and financial journals. In a matter of a few weeks, U.S.I.'s stock responded by being traded more actively and moving up in value. A flurry of interviews and stories appeared. As if from nowhere, U.S.I. became an important company, one with its own following.

As Frank Saunders, who had helped Sonnenberg implement the campaign, observed, "Quite suddenly, the company

ere really something. And what it was doing
ig because somehow U.S. Industries had man-
gether some of the best minds in American in-
a brilliant coup. And it cost them nothing. They
a board and they were going to pay its members
why not get the best for your money?"

nberg, of course, realized that nothing made top
corporate executives and others of high public exposure feel
more appreciated than being invited to join the board of directors of a large company. Within each powerful man, he
knew, there was still a craving for recognition and more power.
No one was too busy or preoccupied for that.

Then again, there was perhaps the greatest feat of all,
simple and stunning in effect, in which Sonnenberg propelled
a struggling former architect who had turned to selling soap
to become the subject of a *Time* magazine cover article. In
retrospect, the accomplishment may not seem so great because Charles Luckman bore the mantle of "Golden Boy" as
far back as his high-school days in Kansas City, accomplishing with ease anything he ever attempted. But, despite that,
if there is one single achievement that public-relations men
today cite Sonnenberg for, it is the media barrage that he engineered for Luckman, beginning with the *Time* cover piece.
That exposure was to cast the subject into national promi-
nence, making him a favorite in the then-Democratic White
House.

It is difficult today, impossible perhaps, except for those
senior citizens with an exceptional memory, to recall the great
stature Luckman attained as a business statesman and critic
and the great impact he made on the public in the last half of
the 1940s. Handsome and lithe, appearing a sort of dignified
Bing Crosby, low-key but articulate, Luckman didn't engen-
der the degree of resentment others more abrasive might have
when occasionally he lambasted, at important meetings,
American industry for its slothful, insulated ways. During his
three-hundred-thousand-dollars-a-year tenure as president of
Lever Brothers' American soap empire, he was reported in the
country's leading newspapers to be under serious consideration by President Harry Truman as chairman of the Atomic
Energy Commission to succeed David Lilienthal. Instead, he
remained at Lever and doubled as Truman's food conserva-

tion administrator, a post that carried him across the country and the Atlantic to make speeches exhorting the public to consume less meat, sugar, and bread and curb a burgeoning worldwide food shortage.

He had wanted to be an architect, he claimed, since he was twelve years old. He had never had another ambition. In fact, when he graduated from high school, he was offered a four-year scholarship to the state university's school of business administration. He insisted, instead, that his only love was architecture.

"I worked like a dog in college and I got top grades, not only in architecture but in engineering," he told Robert S. Bird in a 1955 article in the *New York Herald Tribune*.

> Bill [Pereira] and I must have been the two hardest working fellows in the architectural school. Harriet, who was a student in the university, used to come over to architectural school every night to bring us apples and sandwiches, we were so deep in work. Harriet and I have been together all the way through. I married her the week after I graduated. We didn't have any money but we felt if we waited for that it might be years before we could marry.
>
> So we got married and I had to get a job right away. Bill and I both got offers from an architect's office to work for $16 a week. Bill accepted, but Harriet and I couldn't get along on that salary, so I answered an ad in the newspaper. Colgate wanted a layout man, copy layout, and would pay $24 a week. That was enough for Harriet and me to live on. I took it. And that's when I got sidetracked.
>
> I was brilliant in those days, very brilliant. I told the guy who was my boss that I intended to go into architecture and would be leaving the job in about six months when the depression was over. It took eighteen years for me to get back into architecture. But I don't regret those years.

Luckman had no cause to regret them because he was in his element. Whether it was because of his early zeal to make money or an instinct about how to succeed, he demonstrated almost from the outset with Colgate that he possessed twin abilities. He was naturally creative, and he was a natural salesman. With either attribute, he generated credibility. He rose quickly in the frantically competitive facial-products field, moving out of the advertising department to sales and management, and in his early thirties became the president of the Pepsodent Company. It was there that his and Sonnenberg's paths crossed.

There was some good fortune behind it. Pepsodent was owned by Albert Lasker, who, as mentioned earlier, was a good friend of Sonnenberg and had sometimes served, by the publicist's own assertion, as "my tout." The Lasker-Sonnenberg alliance had warmed over the years, the advertising man appreciating the flair and fine professionalism of the publicity man and vice versa. It reached perhaps its greatest closeness when Lasker entrusted the handling of the transfer of power and, more important, ownership in his big agency, Lord and Thomas, to three of his key associates—Emerson Foote, Fairfax Cone, and Don Belding. They renamed the agency Foote, Cone and Belding, and it became one of the largest and most respected in the advertising field. Lasker was said to have been unusually pleased by the skillful way in which Sonnenberg and his associates handled the media coverage, which appeared to enhance Lasker's desire to be remembered as a philanthropist and business statesman.

Lasker was also enthusiastic about Luckman. He convinced the handsome ex-architect that he was destined for great things but needed some professional help if he were to fulfill his role at Pepsodent and also become known in the most important quarters. Who could do it? Sonnenberg, of course.

Leonard Matt, who worked with the publicist during those years of the mid-forties, tells what happened.

"Ben was hired by Luckman mostly as an ego trip. But it didn't matter because we tackled it as though it were a major corporate program. Three of us spent three days in Chicago at Pepsodent's office getting Luckman's life story from him. And we saw him in action. He was a handsome man, with wavy blond hair, very forceful and magnetic, a spellbinder of a speaker. We wondered, though, if Lasker had convinced Luckman to hire Ben to get publicity for him and his company or to find a buyer for Pepsodent."

It was a question that seemed justified soon after when Lever Brothers & Unilever Ltd. made a bid to buy Pepsodent. Lever, which had headquarters in England and the Netherlands, was the largest company in the world manufacturing soap and margarine. Its American subsidiary was the Lever empire's most important overseas division. But it lacked something that chief competitors like Procter & Gamble and Colgate had—a dentifrice. Pepsodent, however, had its famous toothpaste by that name, which led the field. So Lever plunked down $15 million to buy Pepsodent and in the process got Luckman.

Within a matter of days, the thirty-seven-year-old Luckman was named president of Lever Brothers U.S. His success seemed to be bearing out the "luck" in his name. He had the top job at a company doing $250 million of business a year, had gotten $1.5 million after taxes for his Pepsodent stock, was given a salary of $300,000 a year, one of the largest in the country for a corporate executive. And he had Sonnenberg.

In addition, Luckman had someone else on his payroll who was a character in his own right: a comedian with somewhat bulging temples, a nose that came to a point, a likable smart-aleck manner, and a ready ability with one-liners—Bob Hope. Luckman brought Hope with him to Lever for commercials and television "specials." Hope was considered such an asset for selling Pepsodent that having him under contract was considered a coup.

Sonnenberg, who had already gotten *Time* magazine to do one piece on Luckman, saw an opportunity for another in the same magazine of perhaps greater scope. "Ben worked with Joe Purtell, the business editor of *Time*," Leonard Matt said, "and Purtell agreed to try a cover piece. Did Ben also work through Henry Luce, the owner of *Time* magazine? Personally, I don't know, but I wouldn't be surprised. Sonnenberg worked at various levels at the same time. But Luckman as a cover story, we all thought, was a helluva story and certainly merited it."

The *Time* cover article took up three and a half pages and included six photos, one of Luckman clowning with Hope. The impact was great, one of the most impressive pieces about a businessman anywhere in years. But it was only part of a barrage of stories. *"Newsweek,* the *New York Times,* and the *Herald Tribune* also did major pieces on Luckman," said Leonard Matt. "The publicity kept up, and it was just great."

But, as every public-relations person will admit, there's more to success than media placements. At least as important is keeping the client's ego intact and, in fact, helping to sustain and feed it. Sonnenberg had good connections at the White House through Ben Cohen and Tom Corcoran, and it is likely that President Truman's interest in Luckman was fed by Sonnenberg through his two friends. Sonnenberg was hardly reluctant to tap "the levers of power."

Three years later, when the British owners of Lever Brothers decided to unseat Luckman as their American chief, he had little with which to recriminate Sonnenberg—after all, a publicity man can only do so much—or his superiors. The Lever overlords were apparently distressed that their American cousins had not had the initiative to come up with a detergent at a time when Procter & Gamble's Tide and Colgate's Fab were being snapped up by housewives. More than thirty years later some sources who were involved at the time say that it wasn't Luckman's fault as much as that of his predecessor, Francis A. Countway, an elegant gentleman who acquired a glowing reputation as one of America's greatest advertising men. Countway, the sources say, concentrated more on soaps—Lifebuoy, Lux, and Swan—than on detergents, so that the equipment to mount a campaign in the detergent field just wasn't at hand. Whether or not Countway can be blamed for the detergent fiasco, he will always bear the reputation of having discovered B.O., otherwise known as body odor. Although Lifebuoy had been introduced into the American market in 1898 from England, it was Countway who, after a sweaty golf game one warm afternoon, created B.O. to render Lifebuoy more salable.

After leaving the Lever U.S. headquarters in Cambridge, Massachusetts, Luckman returned to his old love, architecture, and joined his former classmate Bill Pereira as a partner. Again, Luckman found much zest in his new career, designing the new Madison Square Garden in New York and the proposed Pacific Coast Stock Exchange and office building in Los Angeles.

These three seminal cases in Sonnenberg's ever-growing reputation merit some analysis. Each contained the underlying elements that pointed to the increasingly skillful, increasingly Byzantine way he worked.

More and more, it dawned on Sonnenberg that many of the nation's business and government elite needed help in achieving the professional or personal image they wanted. But they woefully misunderstood the media, how these worked and how to approach them. Inevitably, Ben realized, the principle of a free press running smack up against an establishment wanting only to be seen in the best light led to an adversary relationship. The only means of blunting it was to understand the demands and needs of both, to plow smoothly in the gray ground left between the conflict of those demands and needs and hope that the seeds would grow quietly and thrive. But that was only the superficial side of the problem and the solution. The significant factor in all of it was that people, regardless of their status, life style, or income, had a core of insecurity, a need to be bolstered and even emotionally supported. That meant, Ben knew, that catering to a person's self-respect, shoring it up in different ways, would build a friendly, sympathetic reaction toward him, Sonnenberg and his needs, whether it was to help his clients or mold a closer rapport with the press.

The social activities of 19 Gramercy Park helped greatly. Whether the guests headed billion-dollar corporations, sat in Congress or the Senate, or starred in the columns of the nation's most powerful papers, everyone liked an invitation. They came filled with curiosity and even some suspense. The lavishness of the decor, the elegant service from the retainers, and, above all, the host's warmth and interest in them, not to mention the excitement generated by the other celebrated guests, almost always gave pleasure to those who rapped on the lion-headed knocker.

This was not true of everyone, of course. "When I was invited to the Sonnenberg house," said a *New York Times* colleague of mine, "I liked being invited to cocktails, but I felt overwhelmed and not pleasantly. There was so much artwork, so many pieces of brass, so many rooms crowded with culture that I felt it was all too gaudy and intended for effect. But please don't quote me by name."

As for Sonnenberg, the reactions didn't matter so much as his own enjoyment at being able to live the way he wanted to and, in the process, to be able to display it to anyone he wanted to. He had no qualms about using his house and its effects for business purposes, or about his quaint way of dressing. It was him, Ben Sonnenberg. But it was also a vehicle for him to build up his clients' and friends' feeling of recognition, to allow them to enjoy and benefit from participating in his way of life. Ego-trip? Of course. Ego-building for others, even those big businessmen who wondered how their publicist or potential publicist could live so well? Yes.

Sometimes, the task went far beyond the image-building need. In the case of the Rudkins, it began with a loan of three hundred dollars, proceeded to a warm personal relationship and an ongoing publicity assignment, and it made Sonnenberg rich indeed. In the cases of both John Snider of U.S.I. and Charles Luckman of Pepsodent and Lever Brothers, it was a matter of rethinking their perception priorities. Snider moved to another public-relations agency where he felt he would get more attention and Luckman, mildly observing that all of Sonnenberg's efforts hadn't kept him up there, changed careers. In many other cases, however, Sonnenberg and his important clients became friends, and he performed for them favors and social chores that made some grateful for years. Help with spouses, children, or difficult employees are examples of some of these. Assistance in grooming, speech, the social amenities are others. And later, not surprisingly, he even helped the heads of some well-known companies to make mergers that rendered them even bigger and better known.

Later, when the men died, he even helped their widows find a more meaningful existence by devoting their time and money to humanitarian and social causes.

In line with his theory of "the levers of power," he would hardly drop his contacts with the media either at the working level or at the top. He would cement relationships with both, gently prodding each layer either to influence the other or to simply keep the contacts alive. But though it worked well for him, since he knew when to massage and when to probe, he cautioned his clients never to follow suit. "Make the contacts," he urged, "but don't let one know about the other. It's like putting the wrong ends of two wires together. You short circuit."

He knew William Paley, founder and long-time chairman of the Columbia Broadcasting System, and also Walter Cronkite and Dan Rather, CBS's two most visible news luminaries, as well as reporters down the line. Sonnenberg kept his contacts as quiet as he could, although he was seen with them often enough at the 21 Club, Pavillon, and other fine restaurants. But no one knew just what he was doing with or for them.

In an interview, Stanley Marcus, the former chairman of the Neiman-Marcus fashion chain in Dallas, observed, "I learned more from Ben Sonnenberg about life and business than from any person except my father." Marcus, now a management consultant and a prolific author and raconteur about his life and experiences, added, "And Ben would sometimes chide me that I wasn't even a client."

If he had occasional qualms about whether he was being either paid enough or appreciated enough by his blue-chip clients, Sonnenberg nonetheless enjoyed considerable psychic income in those years when he had put it all together. "America's most successful and most colorful public relations man was Ben Sonnenberg," declared Leon Harris in his 1979 book, *Merchant Princes*. "He was paid enormous fees by corporations and individuals because his advice was unorthodox and effective. To Texaco he gave only two shocking suggestions— that it insist upon cleanliness in its rest rooms and that it introduce grand opera to America by means of radio. His most amusing myths and disguises he made for himself, but as one acute observer remarked, there were only two essential things to understand about Sonnenberg: 'The first is that only the most improbable things about him are true; the second, that early in life he discovered that candor is the greatest wile in the world.' "

In regard to the beyond-professional services the publicist rendered for many of his clients, Harris relates an amusing episode involving some of the family problems of Fred Lazarus, Jr. Lazarus, the founder of Federated Department Stores, Cincinnati, the country's largest operator of such stores as Bloomingdale's, Abraham & Straus, Filene's, and Burdine's, was an amiable tyrant whose three sons, Fred III, Ralph, and Maurice ("Mogie"), feared him until the day he died in 1973 in his early eighties.

"Fred's New York publicity agent was the late Ben Sonnenberg," wrote Harris.

A public relations genius whose work, in his own unbuttoned phrase, consisted of "diapering rich men," Sonnenberg succeeded in getting stories about Fred into *Time, Fortune, Saturday Evening Post* and other journals in the 1940s and 1950s—stories that were an important part of building Fred's reputation for being the shrewdest retailer in America. "In what seemed like the middle of the night, Fred once telephoned me and insisted that I immediately come over to his New York apartment," Sonnenberg remembered. "Of course, I was angry but Fred sounded genuinely distressed and besides, the annual retainer I charged Federated was very substantial. On the way over I tried to imagine what was disturbing him so, but nothing I had heard from my friends in Wall Street gave me any clue.

"When I got to his apartment, he did not even greet me but burst out immediately, 'A terrible thing has happened, Ben, just terrible, or I would not have disturbed you at this hour or at least I would have been willing to discuss it on the telephone.'

"Braced for a business tragedy of considerable proportions, I listened without saying a word and suddenly Fred exclaimed, 'It's Mogie! Mogie wants to quit the business. He wants to be a writer!'

"If Mogie had wanted to be a jockey or a pimp, Fred could not have been more horrified. I managed not to laugh and explained that wanting to be a writer and actually becoming one were two different things— that the aberration would probably pass—which it did."

Laughing inwardly about it or not, Sonnenberg increasingly found himself drawn into both the professional and personal affairs of the corporate chiefs among his clients. He knew that despite his efforts to "spend two or three nights a week at home" with his family he wasn't giving its members enough attention or even consideration. Ben, Jr., in particular, was displaying more signs of rebellion. Hilda was disappearing more often from the cocktail parties and dinners that he arranged. Only Helen, his daughter, seemed to understand. Ben was beginning to suffer some serious pangs of guilt.

He wondered at times if his clients and friends weren't taking advantage of him and his good intentions. Did he really need to hold their hands so much and, for that matter, did he really need all those clients? With a growing frequency, he found himself losing interest and even resenting the nitty-gritty of the public-relations business: the releases, the prodding and the following up of the press, the paperwork and routine details that a full P.R. agency required.

But, at least for the time being, he told himself, how could he argue with success, dramatic success, which had created a unique aura around him? There was, in fact, so much more he could do, so many more walls to be scaled, so many others who badly needed him to make them appear better than they were. There was just no time for any doubt.

8

$9,991 FOR KNOWING WHERE TO DO IT

The pangs of guilt wouldn't go away, but his involvement with his clients and his friends—it was hard to separate the two—deepened and widened. Much as he enjoyed it all, he felt more and more that he was in a self-imposed trap. It was a trap, however, with velvet sides and a cushiony bottom, because he loved what he was doing, and "they," his clients, loved him for doing it.

How, for instance, could you not help a "friend" even if he was a client who paid you?

In the summer of 1927, Edwin Goodman, the founder of Bergdorf Goodman, employed Sonnenberg at a hundred dollars a month to provide publicity for the then all custom-made fashion store. As Andrew Goodman, Edwin's son and his successor as Bergdorf's chairman, recalls, "I never could exactly stand Ben, maybe because I was only twenty years old and

Ben dressed oddly, as if he were putting on an act. But Father admired him, especially his *chutzpah*, and my father was a shy man, austere, maybe even forbidding, and I suppose he admired Sonnenberg because he was the opposite.

"I remember that Ben would always come into the store with a book of clippings to show us. He had gotten lots of stories, but they were all in papers like the *Tulsa Gazette* or the *Oklahoma Bugle*, not that those were the real names. But I said to him, 'Ben, what do those crappy clippings mean when we sell only expensive, custom-made clothes? There are only fifteen or twenty thousand people in the whole country who can afford it.' But Father didn't seem to care. He was a softy underneath what some people thought was a stuffy exterior and I guess there was something youthful and awfully vivacious about Ben.

"That summer, Father decided to take a gamble on Ben, who wanted desperately to go to Europe and broaden himself. He gave Ben two thousand dollars, a lot of money in those days, and Ben left. He was gone the entire summer. But when he came back he had two prizes. One day, he appeared in Father's office with them—the Prince Matchabelli, the parfumier, and the Grand Duchess Marie Romanov. He told Father that he had hired them for us to help us gain some new glamor with the public. They would be sort of in-house celebrities, giving us media attention and public prestige. The prince actually was a fine asset; he looked like a prince and he knew perfumes. The duchess actually could have been an important figure—if the monarchy was ever returned to power in Russia—which of course was unlikely.

"But, unhappily, the duchess didn't have the aplomb, the panache, that Prince Matchabelli had. She looked, in fact, like a plain housewife. On Ben's instructions, we used her sort of behind the scenes. We would ask some of our customers, those who might have been born in Russia or Europe, if they would like to meet the Grand Duchess Marie Romanov? Many did, of course, but sometimes it didn't work. One woman from the Bronx told Father afterward, 'Listen, Mr. Goodman. If she's a grand duchess, I'm the Queen of Sheba.' "

The older Mr. Goodman continued to like Sonnenberg for his personality, zeal, and creativity. He would drop the press agent for a while, but would hire him again. The relationship

lasted for well over a quarter-century. For his p
forgot the kindness and confidence that Edwin G.
played toward him, perhaps the European trip as i.
anything. In 1951, when Bergdorf Goodman celebrated it.
tieth anniversary, Sonnenberg pitched in as thought it were a
historic, national event. "The odd thing about Sonnenberg,"
observed Andrew Goodman, "was that if you gave him a proj-
ect to handle, like a fiftieth anniversary, he was simply terrific. But if you put him on a retainer, he did nothing, or practically nothing."

After a number of discussions, the Goodmans and their
publicity agent decided that they should celebrate their fiftieth anniversary with a gala dinner dance at the Plaza Hotel,
which was just across the street on Fifth Avenue and Fifty-
ninth Street. Somehow, Andrew recalls, it was decided that
the guests would pay fifty dollars a person to attend. "But
Father had lots of qualms over that," said Andrew. "I remember him asking us if people would be willing to pay to come
to an anniversary event. We assured him that they would. And
they did. It was a sellout at the Plaza, seven or eight hundred
people. Sonnenberg did the whole thing, and wonderfully,
too."

What the publicist did was typical. Then, as many times
later when he had lunch or dinner with Andrew, he would
arrive with a three-by-five-inch card folded in his pocket and
then take it out to unfurl his ideas. He confided to Andrew,
"That's my business, to dream up ideas. I'll give you a hundred
at a time and ninety-seven will be godawful. But if one is a
good one, it will be worth it."

Ben had several good ideas for the anniversary event. One
was that the dinner dance have not only a fashion show, but
one that people would remember for a long time. A top designer was engaged, and a show was developed, one of the
first to have a scenario, a story—a method that has since become standard. Another Sonnenberg gem was to scatter buckets of authentic-looking gold dust from Bergdorf's Fifty-eighth
Street entrance to the Plaza's steps and lobby. It stopped pedestrians and traffic, too.

Sonnenberg's greatest coup may have been his idea of
having live mannikins in Bergdorf's Fifth Avenue windows. It
might not stop today's shoppers in their tracks, but in 1951 it

was startling. During the Bergdorf fiftieth-anniversary cele-
bration, pedestrians were startled to see what appeared to be
dummies suddenly come alive in the store's windows.

Sonnenberg was convinced that Bergdorf's location was
unique, Andrew Goodman recalled. "He would tell us, 'You've
got something no one would ever have, something they can
never take away from you. Your apartment on top of the store,
the fountain on the Plaza, the horse-and-carriages going back
and forth. Let me tell you this. If you wanted to, you could
invite all the ambassadors in Washington to come to any major event you had and they would. And then you could invite
Fritz Kreisler to come and play his violin. And Ethel Merman
to sing. And also Gypsy Rose Lee to come and entertain in her
way. And they would all be there.' " Recalling it all, Andrew
Goodman ruefully shook his head but smiled, "That was Sonnenberg. He believed in the shock treatment."

Then again, because he would not forget a friend or a
sponsor, he found himself, often reluctantly, responding to the
challenge of reaching someone important when no one else
could. People were impressed with his skill in wielding the
levers of power. More and more of them came to him with
pleas to help them when decisions were being made that were
beyond their control. One such client, the head of an important company, had a major problem with Congress because a
key member whom he had contacted was unable to furnish
the company with the relief it wanted. It was almost the end
of the fifties, a time when seniority on Capitol Hill carried
more weight than it did three decades later. The key member
sat on a committee headed by a tough, aging, hardheaded,
indomitable southerner. The white-maned chairman, a bible-
thumping Baptist and an unflappable Democrat, espoused a
Jeffersonian philosophy, which he interpreted to mean that
the democratic checks were there not only to maintain a balance, but to keep the country morally clean.

"Ben, you've got to help, damn it," the client begged.
"Even if that old bird won't go along, we've got to get his ear
so that we know we've exhausted every possibility."

But the southern congressman was apparently unreach-
able. When he learned of the businessman's efforts to influence him, it only hardened his resolve. Sonnenberg got busy,

and in a week or two he had the solution. He found that he had once helped a man who had an unusually warm relationship with the congressman. It was simply a matter of checking his office and his mental files until he came up with the right power lever. On the phone, the man he had helped promised to do what he could. He met Ben's client and then placed a call to Washington. Later, the grateful individual was in Washington and met the congressman.

Some weeks later, when the committee chairman met Sonnenberg's client, he seemed to have enjoyed the power game in which he had been the target. At least, that may have been why he thumped the client on the back and told him, "You old so-and-so, how in hell did you all figure out the one goshdarned link that would work?"

If Sonnenberg sometimes tired of the detail and the troubles his big corporate clients brought him, he never seemed to weary of befriending and helping talented young people. He was not interested in only being their benefactor because he was always also looking for bright, new people to add to his agency staff. At the same time he sought out the most promising new media writers for future contact on placing stories or for free-lancing special pieces for him. But, once the initial purpose for the relationship was taken care of and he decided he liked the young man, there appeared to be little he wouldn't do for him. To some, he became a friend and even sponsor for several years, and to others he assumed a unique, paternal role that lasted a long time.

Julian Bach, a writer on *Life* magazine and later a well-known literary agent, met Sonnenberg when the publicist was courting not only major media writers, but those who were single and could fill in at the Sonnenberg table at a soiree or dinner. In 1946, recently divorced, Bach was invited to many dinners. Sitting at his desk in the Time-Life Building one afternoon, Bach answered his phone and heard Ben say, "Listen, young man, there's this beautiful movie actress staying at the St. Regis. We are having a small dinner party tonight. How would you feel about escorting her?"

Bach recalls that his heart pounded. The actress was already a legend, although still fairly young, and he had loved her since he was a boy. He readily agreed.

That night, however, he found himself seated next to Ben's daughter, Helen, whereas the actress sat next to Sonnenberg, who monopolized her time.

By the end of 1947, Bach found himself dropped from the Sonnenberg invitation list. "That happened as soon as Ben found out that I was remarrying," Bach said. "He no longer had any use for me."

In 1955, Ben met Carl Spielvogel, a business and financial writer on the *New York Times*, then in his early twenties. Spielvogel later became an advertising columnist for the *Times* and then left the paper to enter the advertising field, becoming one of its greatest success stories. Within a decade, he literally exploded to the top as the chairman-of-the-board of the Interpublic Companies, the largest group of advertising agencies. As the 1980s dawned and a policy split developed at Interpublic, Spielvogel left and formed his own advertising agency, Backer and Spielvogel. It started with one client and soon was one of the hottest "shops" on Madison Avenue.

"I met Ben through a mutual friend and he offered me a job," Spielvogel recalled. "I told Sonnenberg that I really wasn't interested in the public-relations business, but out of that meeting came a very valuable friendship. We used to have lunch and dinner and would talk regularly. He was one of my mentors, and I am a serious believer in the mentor system. There's nothing like it. Ben was always willing to offer advice. And he was always willing to bring two people of different backgrounds together so that good things might come of it.

"I remember one evening in 1958, we sat in his house. He folded his arms and said, 'My boy, I'm going to teach you how to waste time profitably. Most people don't want to waste time profitably. One way is to get to know your client and his problems and the way to do that is to get around, meet lots of people and talk to them.' He would remind me of that often. He would appear at lots of dinners, cocktail parties, and other events and over the years, he told me, the cumulative effect of appearing at all of them taught him how to build a business. 'The object of all of this,' he said, 'is to make yourself available to ideas and businesses.' "

When he reached the age of thirty and decided to change careers by leaving the *Times*, Spielvogel said that he spoke to Sonnenberg about his plans. "He was gracious about giving

me the time to talk about it. 'Go where the oppo
he told me. He taught me that there are a lot of
you feel in your viscera before you feel it in your he
that come up in your gut before you can explain the.
ally.

"But despite all the advice he gave me about going u   r-
ties and dinners," said Spielvogel, "Sonnenberg actually hated
to sit at formal dinners like one that had twelve hundred
diners at the Waldorf. His trick was that he would come to
them for cocktails and sit through the dinner course, then go
to another for the entrée and maybe to a third for coffee—or
just go home and read. He was a voracious reader in his later
years, maybe because he was afraid he would miss something
that was going on around him or around the world.

"He had very keen eyes and he liked to tell stories about
how he and Stanley Marcus would go from shop to shop, see
what they had and tutor themselves. And he'd tell me, 'If you
want to learn something about art or copper or English furniture, you have to shop.' And that's how he would spend many
a Saturday afternoon."

Over the twenty-three years that Spielvogel enjoyed his
friendship with Sonnenberg, one of the warmest traits that he
remembered about the publicist was Ben's "amazing ability
to sit in his library, his tea glass balanced on his knee, and
allow people to confide in him. . . . At lunch or dinner, he
would take out a folded card from his pocket with an at-
tached, tiny pen and reel off a list of things he wanted to talk
about. . . . He had some odd things he did, quirks, like preferring to drink whiskey out of a stem glass, straight, with no
ice. . . ."

There was no one that Spielvogel knew who was "better
at working at the top than Sonnenberg. He was a great student of people and he could always find someone to help him
push the buttons of power." Once, Ben said, and then repeated it often, "Nothing drives a man like the remembrance
of the nagging hunger in his stomach. Knowing that allows
me to differentiate between those who have known it and those
who were born with a silver spoon." Another time, he observed, "One of the basic things to learn about people is that
if you do something for their children, it will mean more to
them than if you had done something for the parent." And

other time, Ben told him, "Always be fiercely loyal to your friends and never, never break any confidence that they made to you."

Spielvogel was hardly the only target of Sonnenberg's endless flow of advice. There were others, many others, especially the younger public-relations men. In 1969, Gershon Kekst, who had just started his own agency after a ten-year association with Ruder & Finn, received a call from a friend who said that Ben Sonnenberg wanted to meet him. Kekst had tea at 19 Gramercy Park and noticed a pile of newspapers in a corner of the library.

"What's that, Ben?" Gershon asked. "Catching up on your reading?"

Sonnenberg put down his glass of tea. "No," he said. "When we used to live down on the East Side, we were quite poor, but it was a good day when we could buy some herring."

"So?"

"That's what we used to wrap the herrings in," Ben said. "Newspapers. Just so I don't forget."

Was Sonnenberg kidding? Kekst assumed he was. But he knew that the older man was deadly serious when he told him the same evening, "Do you know how to handle an editor? Impress the hell out of him." He then told Gershon about a problem that a client had had with an editor at *Fortune* magazine. The magazine editor was a young, brash type who seemed to carry a chip on his shoulder toward businessmen. Ben's client had cooperated on an interview with the editor, but he received the clear impression that the result would be a classic hatchet job of an article.

Relating what happened before the story had been published, Ben said he had phoned the young man.

"Hello," he said. "I'm Ben Sonnenberg. Do you know me?"

"Nope."

"Fine. I'll take care of that."

Within an hour or two, the editor received by messenger an elaborate package containing a dozen sheets. It was a copy of the Geoffrey Hellman article in *The New Yorker*, a literal paean to Sonnenberg, his great repute, and the elaborate way he lived.

The next day, the publicist phoned again. "Now do you know me?" he asked.

The young man's voice was much softer than it was the day before. "Yes, I do," he admitted.

"Fine. Now we can talk. That article you're planning on my client . . ."

After he finished relating the incident, Sonnenberg said, "I had him in the palm of my hand after that. He turned out to be a nice young man, at that."

Ben also advised Kekst, with a smile, "You must always remember something. Tuck in your client at night so that you are the last person he talks to before he sleeps, and then rouse him gently in the morning so that you are the first one he opens his eyes to the next day."

"You're not serious?" said Kekst.

"Yes, I am," Ben said. But his eyes danced.

As he parted that evening, Kekst said, admiringly, "You've got everything, Ben. This gorgeous house, age, experience, wisdom."

Sonnenberg shrugged. "Maybe so. But it all began a long time ago. I was born an old man."

Another public-relations man who understandably asked not to be identified saw the opportunistic side of Sonnenberg.

"Ben would gladly put up ambassadors from other countries in his house," he said, "and then he would invite Wall Street bankers to meet them so that they could make points with the foreigners when they visited their countries. It was just a little service he provided at Gramercy Park."

The P.R. man also remembered when a Balkan monarch spent a few nights at the house and Sonnenberg learned that she had come with little money and only a sketchy wardrobe. He arranged for her to go to Bergdorf Goodman, a client, and be outfitted. While she was there, Ben invited the press to come to Bergdorf's "to meet the Queen."

One of the most intriguing things the P.R. man remembers Sonnenberg doing occurred when Ben's investment account at a famous banking house dwindled over a period of months. One morning, a partner in the bank opened his mail to find a bill from Sonnenberg for a hundred thousand dollars.

"What the hell is this?" the partner asked a colleague. "Do we owe Ben a hundred big ones?"

"No," replied the other man. "That happens to be the amount that Ben's account dropped the last few months. I think he's trying to tell us something."

"You mean he actually wants us to pay him back?"

The other partner shrugged. "Maybe yes, maybe no," he said.

"He's got some kind of balls."

"You didn't know that?"

The bill, of course, was never paid, and it is likely that Sonnenberg didn't expect it to be paid.

Some who knew Sonnenberg well during the late 1950s and particularly during the 1960s began to realize that there was another side to Sonnenberg, one that made them uncomfortable. It was more than just the occasional edge that came through his feistiness, or the times when his zeal for P.R. hype got out of hand. It was a fleeting sense that he had an ulterior motive in certain friendships, that despite the great service he performed for clients he really had a deep disdain for them and that as he grew more important he used people to gain position, power, and money. Although this may be no different than most people feel or behave, although they may try to conceal it, in Sonnenberg's case the realization of the other side of his nature was more jarring because it was so out of character.

The jolly, bubbling, avuncular disposition conflicted with some of the darker elements of his nature. Those elements were more striking, perhaps, when he gave the impression of claiming credit for things he hadn't done. His prepublication dispatch to important people—many of them not clients—of articles about them to appear in major publications was an example. He dropped famous names into conversations, often indicating an intimate friendship with them, which first impressed listeners and then made them wonder. A growing habit of sending unexpected and unwanted bills dismayed some who thought his favors represented a friendship rather than a client relationship. The upshot of some of those confrontations were court suits that Ben filed, which sometimes resulted in out-of-court settlements.

As he got more deeply involved with major clients, found himself engaged in some activities that he scorned whe. performed by lesser publicists. He pimped for some Wall Street bankers, obtaining expensive prostitutes for their pleasure. He didn't like it, but it did, after all, serve two purposes: it satisfied his client's needs and Ben's need to keep them as clients. He sometimes joked about the lengths to which he went to keep his clients happy. It wasn't just a lot of media placements that did it.

Smooth as he was, his opportunism was never far from the surface. Young men from affluent families, whom Ben met through their parents and befriended, were often flattered and intrigued by his attention. But here and there, though their relationship lasted for years, it gradually dawned on them that they were being used, manipulated, that they were being befriended not only because he liked young people, but so he could "hover around a pot of honey," as one of them put it years later.

Frank Weil met Ben Sonnenberg when he was only ten years old and admitted decades later, "I was mesmerized by him." Today, Weil is a well-known Washington attorney, a former government official, and before that a partner at the highly respected Loeb, Rhoades & Company, a leading investment-banking house on Wall Street.

Weil's family had old money, at least some nine decades old, dating back to 1895, when his maternal grandfather, Aaron E. Normand (originally Nusbaum) cashed in years of successful peddling and ice-cream hawking to buy a one-half interest from Richard Sears in the growing firm of Sears Roebuck.

As a child, Frank Weil became aware of Ben Sonnenberg, who met his parents through a mutual friend. "He had a real presence," Weil recollected. "The odd way he dressed, the colorful way he talked, the big limousine he came in—those made a memorable impression on a young boy. I used to think that he was an actor, later I decided that he was just always acting. Both my father and my uncle died when I was still quite young and Ben sort of assumed a father image for me.

"Much later, after I had graduated from law school and joined Loeb Rhoades, I saw Ben constantly. Over one ten-year period, when I had lunch, cocktails, or dinner with him, I must him thirty times a year. I was one of between young guys that he espoused, all young men ...st of them well-fixed as I was, but Ben always ...ive behind his sponsorship. I have run into at least ...ozen people like me, Sonnenberg protegées, and all of ...em told me that they had had the same, unhappy, final experience with him, a bad conclusion to their relationship."

Weil, a tall, strapping, vigorous man in his early fifties, stared solemnly at his interviewer. "Sonnenberg," he said, slowly, "was the most interesting man I ever met, but he was one of the most opportunistic I ever met."

He explained that he meant that Sonnenberg often appeared to have an ulterior motive behind gestures and favors he granted others. In addition, he and a number of clients whom he influenced most or was most influenced by were imbued with *le droit de seigneur*, the conviction that the power belonged to the elite. "That's why John Loeb, Sr., the head of Loeb Rhoades, never wanted any partners, although he had to accept some because of the money and the clients they brought in, and why Sonnenberg treated his own staff in a hand's off way, as though he were lord of the castle." The publicist also seemed to have an instinct for finding people of wealth who would respond positively to him—men, women, and especially the young men who might have required an older hand outside their families to guide them. "He had known my parents," Weil said, "and I suppose that when my father passed on he felt I needed a substitute. I did, too, and I thought he was a sort of uncle, only it all wound up badly."

Sonnenberg, too, was "an advocate of using the so-called 'back channel' to get things done that could not be easily accomplished by going through regular channels," said Weil. "Back channel," in the terminology of Washington, D.C., where it apparently originated, had come into much use by politicians, diplomats, and security people who worked the official channels while depending more on results through unofficial channels. "Ben loved that system," Weil said, "because it suited him and gave him a chance to pull strings."

Influenced by his mentor, Weil said he tried to get on with the sometimes crusty John Loeb, the senior partner in Loeb Rhoades, by using Ben as his "back channel." The young investment banker needed help, at that, since he wasn't getting on well with his older, senior partner. In 1964, following the collapse of the Wall Street house of Ira Haupt and Company because of the salad-oil kiting swindle, Weil spoke up with concern at a meeting of the Loeb Rhoades partners:

"John, what procedures do we have to safeguard ourselves from a disaster like Ira Haupt's?"

Loeb turned angrily on Weil, aware that all the eyes and ears in the room were on both of them. "If you don't have faith in me," Loeb snapped, "you shouldn't be a partner of mine!"

Later, Loeb called Weil into his office. The legendary investment banker appeared chastened, but his back was still stiff. "Frank, some of our co-partners have disagreed with me," said Loeb, "and say that I should apologize to you. I hereby apologize."

Knowing that Loeb was still peeved, Weil told Sonnenberg about it. Ben's immediate response was to expel a blast of breath through his lips. "Karoom!" he said. "In other words, pow!"

Sonnenberg, Frank had learned, liked to make the analogy that life was like billiards. You propel a ball hard against the others, "Karoom!" and they take off in all directions, some falling where you want them and most not. Finesse and control were what was needed. And especially a clear goal.

"I'll talk to John," Ben said confidently. But nothing happened. Though he asked Ben about it repeatedly, and the publicist told him he was taking care of it "through back channels," nothing occurred that improved his relationship with Loeb until he left. "Ben was obviously giving me the business," Weil said, "or his role as an *eminence gris* with John Loeb was exaggerated. Or perhaps it was their *droit de seigneur* mentality, a belief in the inviolability of family wealth or confined ownership, which was odd in Ben's case coming from such a poor background." In other words, Weil was being told by Ben's silence that Loeb could do what he wanted—even to remain indefinitely offended by him—because of his rank, money, and family connection.

Despite his exhortations to others about keeping confidences, Sonnenberg loved to gossip, Weil said, and "he would disclose confidences but always to what he thought was a discreet audience, and that's something you can never tell for sure. But I admit that I would like to hear the gossip and pass on some of my own. He was always full of questions, like 'What's going on on Wall Street? . . . Who's fucking whom at Lehman Brothers? . . . What kind of deal is Stanley Marcus cooking up? . . .' "

Weil said it dawned on him as he matured that "Ben was using me as he was other younger men. He was no doubt stimulated by them, by getting a peek into their world, but he was evidently as much interested in what he could gain from the connection. As one example, I put him into a few deals, and he made some money out of them. But there was much more he was tucking . . . into that head of his. . . ."

The conclusion to their long relationship developed unexpectedly. While still at Loeb Rhoades, Weil also served as chief executive officer of the Abacus Company, a financial venture firm 44 percent of which was owned by his family. It became involved in a number of investment moves and "I talked to Ben about them as we talked about lots of other things, always as friends and never as part of a client relationship. All Ben ever did professionally was to send out one press release. As things developed, there was a proxy fight by others to try to take over Abacus and I won it. I remember Ben telling me at about the same time the old $9–$9,991 story. You never heard it? It goes something like this: A businessman with a big factory told a friend of his, who happened to be an engineering professor at a university, that he was having problems with the smokestack at his plant. 'Let's take a look at it,' said the professor. They drove up there and the professor got out on the roof, studied the stack and took a hammer out of his coat and banged on it. Immediately, the stack began to smoke as it should. The next day, the factory owner got a bill from his friend for $10,000. 'What the hell is the bill for? I thought we were friends,' demanded the owner.

" 'It's $9 for tapping the stack,' the professor said, 'and $9,991 for knowing where to do it.' "

Shortly after, when Weil had won the proxy fight, he received a bill from Sonnenberg for seventy-five thousand dollars "for services rendered." Said Weil, "I was stunned. Ben had done nothing but the single release, while I had done much more for him by putting him into some deals. 'What kind of a friend are you?' I asked him. I said that I was embarrassed.

'Our lawyers haven't charged us anything like that and that was a professional arrangement.'

" 'I'll have to sue,' Ben warned.

" 'You do that,' I told him. 'I'll defend it myself. I will make a fool out of you.' "

Weil said he didn't pay the bill and Sonnenberg didn't sue. Not, that is, until soon after, in 1972, when Abacus was being merged into Paine Webber Jackson and Curtis, a large stock-brokerage and venture company. Ben decided to file suit against Abacus for the seventy-five-thousand-dollar fee. "I held firm, but the Paine Webber people decided after the merger to settle the thing as a nuisance and Ben got twenty-five thousand dollars. It was like him. He would always get something on someone, wait for a sensitive moment, and then zoom in. During our last talk, I had told him, 'Ben, you're a bad guy.' It was a bad scene. I'll never forget his face, white, quivering. . . ."

Several years later, in the mid-1970s, when Sonnenberg was a lonely man, beginning to get sick and his family away, he would "sit down at his telephone at Gramercy Park on Christmas Eve or New Year's Eve and phone people he knew." Weil said, "I tried to phone him several times after our big fight. I really loved the guy despite everything else. He would never take any of my calls."

They never saw each other again.

9

HERE AND ABROAD, WITH A CLOSE FRIEND

Ben liked going abroad, whether with Alistair Cooke or Brendan Gill, his two closest friends. In one sense it meant getting away from the pressures, the burdens that often followed him home or crowded his desk at 247 Park Avenue. But, in another sense, it was a voyage to his imagination. Even if he had never been there before, it was as if he were coming back.

Sonnenberg and Cooke were a striking pair. Sonnenberg, the short, plump American who was trying to be more British than the British, striding along with his derby, chesterfield, and cane. Alistair Cooke, the famous chief correspondent of the *Manchester Guardian*, English to the core, tall, lanky, easygoing, dressed in the relaxed style of an English country squire. Despite their different approaches, they were closely attuned to each other, mutually appreciative, and they remained loyal friends for over thirty years.

"So far as I could ever tell, Ben was completely unmusical," Alistair Cooke recalled, "but he was a very visual person and his passions for domestic architecture and early eighteenth-century English furniture—Queen Anne, most of all—were genuine. On various trips in England and Scotland, he knew exactly where the best antique shops were: a walnut expert in Gloucestershire, a William and Mary man in Sussex, a Georgian collector in Edinburgh, and always a special man in London to warn him off buying anything with the slightest flaw."

On those trips, Cooke would allow Sonnenberg to take care of the luxuries he had come to expect, "the car and the chauffeur, for example. But he always deferred graciously to my insistence that I should otherwise pay my own way, the hotel bill, train fares, and so on. Ben always had to stay in the best hotels, and sometimes this involved a tricky challenge to his *savoir faire* and to my ingenuity, because he scorned the idea of ever making reservations in advance. If I hinted that the Ritz or the Gleneagles, or whatever, might be full up, he would wave me away with the assurance: 'My dear boy, just relax. You just show up, and there's always a place.' "

Sometimes, his friend's confidence in his own prescience would cause the otherwise unflappable Cooke to scramble.

"Once in Brighton, I discovered by some hectic telephoning that a Labor Party conference had packed the town," Cooke said. "I thumbed through the directories and found a couple of rooms in a rather seedy hotel where, however, Dickens had stayed. I knew that would do it. It did. He didn't mind the threadbare Persian carpets or the fact that he had to walk fifty yards to the bathroom. A plaque commemorating Dickens's stay there sanctified the place for him. 'Anyway,' said Ben, 'you should have seen some of the dumps I stayed in when I was in Michigan in my teens, selling frames for family photographs door to door.' "

On the same trip, Cooke and Sonnenberg went down to Cornwall, but the Englishman again prepared for the visit.

"I had secretly booked our rooms a week ahead," said Cooke, "in a fine eighteenth-century mansion converted into a hotel, where the grounds had been designed by 'Capability'

Brown." Lancelot "Capability" Brown had been a great land-scape architect. Starting his work as a mere gardener, he had displayed such imagination for landscape effects that he had become not only the most respected English landscape archi-tect of the mid-eighteenth century, but was also considered an oracle in all rural improvements, horticultural, agricul-tural, and architectural. His manner of emphasizing both the details and the sweep of the landscape caused him to be widely copied. Cooke knew it would all appeal greatly to Sonnen-berg. But sensing that Ben would be pleased if they could just walk in and be accommodated, Cooke said nothing about the reservation he had made.

"When we got off the train," Cooke related, "Ben again told me that all I had to do was to go into a nearby telephone booth and call the hotel of my choice. I did so and came back to say, 'All is well.' 'You see?' said Ben. 'You fret too much.'

"When we drove up to the place where I told Ben that 'Capability' Brown had designed the grounds, we found that they had been turned into a nine-hole golf course. Ben had never played golf in his life.

" 'You rascal,' said Ben with a chuckle.

" 'Well,' I said, 'look at it this way—this is the only golf course in England designed by Capability Brown.' "

Cooke and Sonnenberg were probably ideal traveling companions because they were ideal friends. They met first in 1948 at a party John Gunther, the author and journalist, and his wife gave for Anthony West, the son of Rebecca West and H. G. Wells. The event, which was held at the Gunthers' home in the East Sixties in Manhattan, was one of "those meander-ing cocktail parties where nobody spends much time with anybody. My wife, Jane, spent more time than I did talking to that strange, little man. He took to her and adored her for the rest of his life."

The next time they met, Alistair Cooke saw Sonnenberg in a different light. "This short, fat man in a derby and a four-button coat was very entertaining, very strange, and a total original. I discovered that he made it a point to be original." Over the years, as their friendship flourished, Cooke found that his own facile "verbal" memory allowed him to remember hundreds of Ben's most original lines. Many had a particular pertinence and a neat bite. Some were self-revealing, but most described Ben's increasingly pungent attitude toward people.

Some years later, Cooke and Ben went down to Palm Beach for a week and spent some time walking the beach. Other than giving a sort of friendly wave to the Atlantic and acknowledging the general balminess by wearing a straw hat, Sonnenberg had on a brown suit with a four-button jacket, enormous hard cuffs and cuff links with emblems of Roman emperors the size of silver dollars. By that time, their friendship had advanced to the point where they could indulge in some prolonged, mutual kidding and neither would feel hurt by it. Ben did it often to Cooke, but now it was Cooke's turn.

"Ben, you know, it's very moving to see the enormous concession you make to the beach," Cooke said. "You do know that you have got on a straw hat, don't you?"

Very slowly and deliberately, Ben said, "My dear boy, when I was about eighteen, I looked in the mirror and I saw that I wasn't pretty. And then I realized that to cut a swath in this world you have to establish a special identity. I further realized that the essential, er, mucilage of a public personality is consistency. If you wear a four-button suit on Park Avenue, you wear a four-button suit at the beach."

Cooke was also amused to learn that he could almost always guess who Ben's newest corporate client was from the metaphors the publicist suddenly began using.

"For me, it became one of the most interesting things to see in Ben," Cooke said. "He handled the language like nobody else in his ironic, oblique way. But if he started talking about the 'long haul' or a 'deadhead' (a nonpaying passenger), you knew that he had Greyhound buses as a client. And if he stopped using those terms, you suspected that he had lost the account."

And then came the day when Sonnenberg stopped being a neophyte about the stock market and started using financial and securities terms. "Ben, do you think that that girl who appeared in the show we saw last night will ever be a star?" Cooke asked one night. Replied Ben, "I don't know about that, but the whole thing has got very much the plot of a proxy fight." Then he would elaborate and Cooke would know that his friend had just learned about proxy fights. Or Ben might be talking about someone getting a divorce and he would say,

"This guy thought he had a growth stock going with that girl. But all he had was a short sale."

Their professional careers grew as their friendship matured. All those years, Cooke continued to report in polished detail for the *Guardian*, then became a well-known personality first on the "Omnibus" television programs and then on public television broadcasting. It was his books that first brought him to Sonnenberg's attention, but it was Cooke's obvious intelligence and culture that endeared him to the publicist.

Both the Sonnenbergs and the Cookes became fond of each other. From 1960 on, it was "a rare week that we didn't see Ben with or without Hilda, and when I was a summer bachelor and he was, too, we would have dinner always on Sunday," Cooke recalled. In the winters, there were the Sunday night movies on the fifth floor of the Sonnenberg house. A core group would be invited to dinner, as many as twelve, and then at least that many more would come in later, the entire group moving upstairs to see the movie. "He would give these large parties certainly through the 1950s," Cooke said. "I always was amazed at the sheer energy of the man, especially since he got up so early every day and forged ahead all day and into the night. The energy of that man with that physique! And he took little exercise. But he continued that pace through the 1950s and into the 1960s."

Aside from their friendship, as an observer of Americana Alistair Cooke was admittedly fascinated by Ben Sonnenberg's immigrant background and the wary, cynical humor that had sprung from it.

"Ben had a marvelous sense of humor," Cooke said. "When people say to me, 'Who do you know who can handle the English language best?' they always expect me to cite an author. I'd tell them, 'Sid [S. J.] Perelman sometimes talked the way he wrote and James Thurber always did. But Ben Sonnenberg beat them all.' Strangely, though, he couldn't write a funny letter. His language came out heavy and contrived when he tried to put it on paper. His talk was something else. I don't know anybody who had his command of the language. It was an elaborate dead-pan form of irony expressed in a language that mixed different vocabularies."

Sonnenberg's humor reflects his own evolution, filtered

through the sieve of his picaresque personality. A story Alistair Cooke tells involves a scholar friend of his who once stayed with him in Cooke's Fifth Avenue apartment. The phone rang that summer evening and Cooke answered.

"What are you doing Tuesday night?" Ben asked.

"I'm not doing a thing."

"Well, let's dine together—"

"I would very much like to, but I have a friend staying with me."

"Bring him along."

"Fine. Where shall we eat?"

"I've discovered a little trattoria, with checked tablecloths and guttering candles," Ben said. "But I understand that the food is bearable."

"Really? What's it called?"

Ben hesitated and Cooke felt his antennae begin to tingle. "It's called 'The Colony,' " said Ben.

The Colony was one of the finest, most fashionable restaurants in Manhattan.

When they sat down together in The Colony, Cooke studied Ben and his academic friend for a moment. He realized that the two minds behind the faces before him represented polar opposites. Ben, of course, was Ben. But the professor was an intellectual man, very articulate and also very Teutonic, an academician who, Cooke said, "constructed his thoughts like an architect, a noun, a verb, a qualifying adverb and so on." To the best of his knowledge, the professor had lived the sort of cloistered existence in which he had never been exposed to an Eastern European mentality, certainly to no one with Sonnenberg's mixture of Slavic and American backgrounds.

As Ben spoke of small things, trying to warm up the atmosphere, the professor stared at him with growing disbelief. Midway through the meal, however, Cooke saw that neither were comfortable yet. The gap between them was too great. And so, attempting to create a bridge, Cooke asked them about a man whom both might know, a famous broadcasting executive.

"Oh, yes, I know him," the professor said. "Do you know him, Sonnenberg?"

"Do I know him? I know him from way back."

The professor, obviously trying to fit into Ben's idiom, said, "I think he is what you would call a smooth operator, wouldn't you say?"

Ben thought a moment. "Well, he's got blue eyes," he said, "and a Scandinavian forelock, and four children. But as far as I am concerned, he's still a virgin."

Silence fell heavily over the checkered tablecloth. It was evident that the professor was totally thrown.

"You see, Professor," Ben said, "I always judge a man, especially if he is in any position of power, according to the glint in his eye in relation to the distance from Budapest, because where I come from Budapest is the Greenwich mean time of all chicanery."

What Ben was saying, in effect, was that he could never understand the well-known broadcasting executive. In other words, Sonnenberg could handle a Persian rug dealer, an important politician, or a big corporate client. He was at home with them, but he wasn't at home with a Scandinavian forelock.

Sonnenberg's touch with the language, the racy roll of his favorite expressions, frequently, however, didn't come out properly in the retelling. Was it hard to recapture an original? Cooke smiled, observing, "I've been favored by this verbal thing of mine, so much so that very often when people quoted something that Sonnenberg said, it made me groan to see that they didn't have it: the flavor, the style of the man. They produced a very crude paraphrase. Ben loved the cadence of a sentence. He could puff out a thing, play with it and then toss in an outrageous punchline. But he had enormous shrewdness. He's the greatest missing character in Balzac."

An incident that Alistair Cooke vividly remembers happened in the first few days after *The Fantastiks*, one of the New York theater's longest-running shows, ended its previews and formally opened in lower Manhattan. It was being presented in a tiny theater holding about fifty-five people. As usual, Sonnenberg had taken two seats on the aisle to ensure a quick, quiet getaway after the first act, should that be necessary.

During the intermission, Ben and Cooke walked out on the street and stood in front of the theater. "What do you think of it?" asked Ben.

"It's awful thin stuff," Cooke observed.

"Do you want to—?"

"Oh, no, no, Ben. I'm your guest. Whatever you want to do, but—maybe we ought to see it through."

"My dear boy," said Sonnenberg. "I was brought up about three streets from here and you know my mother used to tell me that you have got to finish your plate. I learned years ago that you do *not* have to finish your plate." They took a cab and within fifteen minutes they were having supper at 21.

10

NO MORE OVERSHOES

Jim Bowling, the communications chief at Philip Morris, Inc., sent up clouds of cigarette smoke. If one of them had taken the shape of a question-mark, it would have been appropriate. Always a puffing advertisement for his company, the slim, gracious southerner chain-smoked, trying to concentrate on his work. But he couldn't. He stared aimlessly at the plaques that littered his wall, the tobacco industry testimonials, the official appointment as a Kentucky colonel, the tokens of appreciation from the various southern chambers of commerce. They were his rewards for a life devoted to corporate-civic communications. Much of his effectiveness had involved putting out brush fires, even some forest fires, figuratively speaking of course. But they were nothing like the problem that rankled him that morning. It was not only professional, but deeply personal, too.

After an unproductive hour, he tapped the intercom and said to his secretary, "Get me Ben Sonnenberg."

A few moments later, the warm voice of Jeanette Blader, Sonnenberg's longtime secretary, came on. "Ben's not in right now, Jim," she said.

Something in her voice, a trace of breathlessness, stirred him. "What's the matter, Jeanette? Something wrong? Where is he?"

"Nothing's wrong," she said. "Except that we found out for sure this morning that 247 is being torn down. Ben is out looking for new space."

"I see. Have you heard from him? Did he find anything?"

Jeanette's tone went suddenly from breathless to somber. "He called a few minutes ago," she replied. "He was just over at the new Pan Am Building, and he couldn't believe the rentals. Astronomical. You know, he hasn't had to look at new space for twenty-five years. He just couldn't believe what they are asking."

Jim puffed away a moment or two. "When will he get back to the office?"

"After lunch."

"Would you tell him, please, that I would like to come over about two-thirty?"

That bright, fall afternoon in 1963, the short walk from Philip Morris's offices at 100 Park Avenue to 247 Park Avenue could have been pleasant. But Bowling's insides were twisted with uncertainty and concern and, yes, he admitted, fear. How could he tell one of his dearest friends that Philip Morris, which had grown in substantial part due to that friend's great efforts, was going to have to dispense with most, if not all, of his services? The bitter part was that it wasn't because Ben's skills were fading—not at all—as much as it was that Ben had lost interest in the day-to-day operations of the agency. Jim knew that there were people working for Sonnenberg whom he had literally not met. Philip Morris was growing steadily and needed the daily services of a P.R. agency that could function as a direct reflection of the company's growth. But Ben, as Bowling well knew, was very busy in other ways, doing the things he enjoyed and running the agency with his left hand, if that. He simply wasn't interested any longer in the mundane, day-to-day details required in servicing a major account. Bowling had been building up to telling Ben the realities of the situation for weeks. Although he dreaded hurting Ben's feelings, he realized that the news that day that the building would be torn down offered the perfect opportunity to do what was necessary. He had discussed the inevitability of it with George Weissman, another senior Philip Morris executive. Low-keyed but brilliant, Weissman, who was being pushed as an eventual company president, ironically, had even worked for Ben in the agency not so many years ago.

When Jim arrived, Sonnenberg was sitting at his huge, empty, shining desk, drinking a glass of tea, and taking some phone calls. Jim was always amazed at how the publicist, whether in his office or in his home, could manipulate three, four, or five phone conversations at a time, forcing Jeanette to maneuver multiple holds. Sonnenberg looked jaunty, greeting Bowling with a wave and a grin. Finally, he concluded his last call with a verbal flourish and "take good care of yourself, young man." The "young man" usually meant that he was talking at least to a contemporary and quite possibly to an older man. Now he turned and gave Jim Bowling his full attention.

Somehow, recalls Bowling, they got off immediately on a discussion of an investment Ben had made. Then Sonnenberg reached into a drawer and pulled out a spiral book, his "portfolio," which contained a list of his investments and how they had fared. "Of course, Pepperidge Farm is my crown jewel in the portfolio," said Sonnenberg, "and it gives me a peculiar satisfaction that as I work to enhance the image of that company, to polish its escutcheon, I am also improving its capital appreciation so that Benjamin Sonnenberg also profits."

The roly-poly man with the tight collar and the walrus mustache continued to elaborate in that vein, and Bowling found himself chafing and waiting impatiently for the right moment to break in with his message. Finally, when Ben leaned back in his high chair and raised the glass to his lips, Jim plunged in. As he remembers it, he spoke nervously and anxiously, the words and sentences pouring forth in an uninterrupted monologue, unlike his usual well-modulated manner.

"You know, Ben, there are people working for you you don't know. They aren't capable of providing the quality performance that's always been your hallmark. What they are doing, in effect, is really trading on your name and your reputation, which is not necessarily long-term in your best interest, nor would you necessarily approve all these people and the way they work. I wonder if you shouldn't consider taking a different role. I wonder if the time hasn't come when you might not consider concentrating on what you are really doing. Spending more time counseling top management, counseling wealthy individuals, finding members of boards of directors for companies—all that has nothing much to do with that old public-relations operations that is still operating under your name. Now, I understand you are looking for new office space. That means you are contemplating change. Isn't this the right time . . . ?"

Sonnenberg put down the glass. He directed a searching glance at his old friend-client, tried to smile, but couldn't. He swallowed, the pink pouches of his cheeks crinkling, and Jim thought he could detect some pain working its way behind the walrus mustache. They quietly regarded one another as the traffic noise of Park Avenue drifted up to them.

The matter, they both knew, wasn't a new one. It had come up before in wisps and hints, such as at a luncheon Ben had had with John Scott Fones at the Pavillon two years before when for the first time he had allowed some indication of his eventual plans. It had not been a pleasant luncheon because Fones, who was probably his top man at that point, had taken the initiative.

As Fones related it, "It was in the spring of 1961. As Ben's senior associate, I couldn't help looking ahead to what could or might happen. I sat in Montego Bay on a little vacation and decided that I would write a five-year plan for the agency. He had sort of hinted around that he might want to retire, and I decided that I would take over, run it operationally, and maybe have him available as a client-getter and be available for meetings with them. I hired a public stenographer in Montego and came back to New York and told Ben I had something important to talk to him about.

"At the Pavillon, I spread my twelve-and-a-half-page memo out in front of him. I knew that he preferred memos of only a paragraph or a page at most. But I wanted to spell it out—the future for the agency—because I felt he would respond to our continuing it and even expanding it. But I was wrong, dead wrong. He read the first few pages, flicked through the remainder, and then suggested we order lunch. And then he told me that he would close the agency, no one would take it over. It wouldn't happen right away, but over the next few years. That's when I decided to go into business for myself. . . ."

Did Ben explain his decision? Fones was asked. "No," he said, "except that it was pretty clear to me after all those years that Sonnenberg was a private guy who, when his particular tap dance was over, would want the curtain to close, and that would be the end of that. He had had his day in the spotlight, and when the spotlight went out it's all over. It might have been a selfish way of looking at it, but I could understand it. He probably didn't want his name on an agency that someone else would run but not in the Sonnenberg manner. I think that if a clone had come along who was twenty years younger . . ."

Amid this strangely satisfying hum and clatter of the Park Avenue traffic, muted as it was, Ben was still staring at Bowling. Jim's breathless words and Jack Fones's hurt and disappointed reaction mingled in Sonnenberg's ears. He felt the painful edge of reality. They were both right. Philip Morris needed a full-time, motivated agency to serve it daily. Jack Fones needed a goal so that he could reach greater heights. Sonnenberg had been in their way. And there was something else that gave a cause for pain. George Schreiber, an alter ego if ever there was one, was ill, terminally ill. Brain tumor. Ben took a deep breath. The pain eased a bit. It was clearly time for a change, one that he had been building to for some time, only now circumstances had taken over. Gently stroking his mustache, Ben said, "Young man, I think you've got something."

It was all neatly arranged. Philip Morris was to be generous. The top brass, led by Weissman and Bowling, had cleverly worked out an arrangement whereby it would treat the Sonnenberg staff as if its members were its own employees in terms of severance and related matters. As Bowling related later, "They were taken care of, very well, very generously. We did, after all, have a thirty-year relationship with the agency." As for Sonnenberg himself, after he had graciously agreed with Bowling that running the agency didn't interest him anymore, that he was doing other things that he found more fun and more rewarding, they talked it out and Bowling suggested that Ben might get a retainer so that he could be a consultant. Philip Morris would get itself another agency for the daily, ongoing matters. It was quite a change. Philip Morris was Sonnenberg's biggest client.

Bowling walked slowly back to his office, his emotions mixed. He realized that the one thing that they hadn't worked out was what, if anything, the two of them should say publicly about his change in life or his change in the agency. It was only a short walk, but as Bowling entered his office the telephone was ringing, and his secretary told him on the intercom that it was a *New York Times* columnist calling for a comment from Philip Morris about Ben Sonnenberg. In that brief, eight-minute walk, Bowling realized that Ben had phoned the *Times* to announce he was changing his life and that he was phasing out the public relations agency so that he would become a consultant.

Only, as Jim learned later, Sonnenberg had done it all in a very adroit way. He simply told the *Times* columnist, "I no longer want to run around in the rain and have to worry about where my rubbers are or my overshoes are to keep my feet from getting wet. Now, I am going to concentrate on a different part of my work and life and I won't have the public-relations aspect anymore or the press activities aspects, you see. . . ."

That, as Bowling related, "got a very different kind of write-up than obviously a flat-out, dull announcement would. Instead, the report was an upbeat thing rather than what could have been an end-of-an-era, downbeat thing. And it worked splendidly."

But there had been another, earlier conversation, several, in fact, that neither Jim Bowling nor Jack Fones had known about, which had swayed Ben into the new direction. They were with Alistair Cooke. The first talk had been in 1961 when Ben and Alistair had been invited to a buffet party at the Riverdale estate of a prominent steel tycoon. There were at least fifty people scattered over the great lawn, drinking and beginning to cluster around the buffet tables. It started to rain, very gently, causing everyone to shuffle into the house. Ben did, too, and then realized that Alistair Cooke wasn't following him as he had thought. Turning, he saw that Cooke had sat down on the lawn and was calmly smoking a cigarette in the drizzle.

"What in heaven's name are you doing?" Ben demanded, walking back and standing over Alistair. "Don't you know it's raining?"

"Of course I know it's raining. But I am an Englishman, in case you've forgotten. A gentle rain like this is like no rain at all to us."

Ben grinned and sank down on the lawn beside him. They spoke for a while about things each man was involved in. Ben observed how busy he was, including evenings spent with clients. Alistair chided him, in a kidding manner, about devoting his precious leisure time with the chairman of, say, Texas Oil, or the president of, say, Brazilian Traction. "Doesn't there come a time," Cooke said, "when you say this is *my* time? Instead, I'll have him to breakfast."

Ben shrugged. "Well, you know," he said, "some people have to earn a dime." Then he quickly became serious. "You mean to tell me that you get up in the morning and you don't get dressed right away but put on a bathrobe and laze around for an hour or two?"

"That's right," said Cooke.

"Then you have breakfast and read the papers and make a few telephone calls—and then you sit down and write what you damn please?"

"That's right," Cooke repeated.

"Don't you get any instructions ever?"

"I never get instructions from the *Guardian*. At one o'clock I telephone Manchester and give them my copy, and the rest of the day is mine."

Ben, stroking his mustache, said, "Gee whiz. You're your own man." It was a revelation.

Even before he gave up the agency, Sonnenberg began to heed Alistair Cooke's advice. After that conversation on the wet, Riverdale lawn, Ben would call Alistair and ask, "What are you up to?" Cooke would reply. "Not a thing. I thought you were having that fellow from Oklahoma over tonight."

"What!" Ben would squeal in mock outrage. "Do you think I'm going to spend the rest of my evenings with tycoons?"

And then Ben came to the point when he was not only no longer having any business meetings—social events at the house were something else—but he was, according to Alistair Cooke, "terribly proud of it."

And when, later, Ben told Cooke, "A lot of those things could be taken care of the next morning. I mean, why can't I sit down in my library instead, have my glass of tea, and read Dr. Samuel Johnson?" it was obvious that Ben was on a threshold.

After that, Cooke knew, it would not be long before Ben took the final step, complete independence, in his own style.

He was all alone now, a one-man band.

After thirty-six years of steadily hustling to build an increasing volume of business, he had embarked on a totally different path. He would divest himself, in fact, he had to, of those accounts that required a public-relations agency or a press agent. Instead, he would become strictly a consultant, primarily of communications but also of corporate and even social behavior. Although he had been inclining toward that shift in roles for some years, actually doing so was difficult, and it made him edgy. Many people didn't understand it, others were convinced he was just throwing in the towel, others that he was getting old.

He took a small office at 280 Park Avenue, where he conducted his new, reduced business. He continued his normal routine, however—the daily lunches, shopping tours, afternoon meetings either at the new offices or at 19 Gramercy Park, but fewer evening soirees and meetings. It pleased him that he was still in demand, and, maybe, even more so, judging by the feelers and contacts that came his way. Just as his new role required certain adjustments on his part, so he found that he had to face the question of whether he would have to change certain habits, those that had worked for him all those years but had also given him problems.

One such habit in question was that of concentrating almost exclusively on working only at the top. That meant that he would rarely contact anyone at a major corporation other than the chairman-of-the-board, the chief executive, or the president. If an assistant got on the phone to take Ben's call, that individual would summarily find himself cut off. If a secretary intervened when he appeared for an appointment, Ben would be gracious, but his manner, however jovial, clearly said he did not like to be kept waiting for the boss. If a less than senior officer phoned or appeared without invitation, he would find it more difficult to get through to Sonnenberg than to his own chief executive officer. It was the *le droit de seigneur* mentality all over, and like every authoritarian premise it occasionally got him into trouble.

There was no better example than what had happened at U.S. Industries, the company that he himself had suggested change its name from the Pressed Steel Car Company and for which he had created the successful concept of owning a "billion-dollar board." It was true that some people at the time had scoffed that all he had done was successfully enlist a bunch of tired, faded men well past their peak or prime, although still well known to the public. The same skeptics had sniped at the "billion-dollar board" label as a hard-to-swallow euphemism. But the financial community had become attentive, and the general public had been impressed. On the other hand, Sonnenberg's insistence on dealing only with chairman John I. Snider and giving Snider's underlings the back of his hand—with a friendly smile, of course—had created resentment within the U.S.I. bureaucracy, and more than a few of its members were waiting for an opportunity to trip him up. It came, too, when Ben least expected it.

Always an opportunist, he found an advertising agency for a subsidiary of U.S. Industries and because of it accepted a "forwarding fee" from the ad agency. It was described by one source familiar with it as of "significant" proportions. Seen in its harshest light, it was a form of a kickback; in its purest light, as a commission. After all, attorneys and physicians get a percentage of the fee when they recommend one another. Why shouldn't a consultant who recommends an advertising agency? Nor was it illegal. But it gave the executives waiting around the bend for Sonnenberg the opportunity to ambush him. John Snider was informed of the transaction by one or more people on his staff, and he summarily fired Ben.

The explanation that some gave afterward—and Sonnenberg believed it—was that Snider wouldn't have been upset about it at all if Ben had simply told him about it himself. But then nothing is that simple. Perhaps Snider had been "out" to get Ben himself for some long-festering reason? Or had he been infected by an oust-Sonnenberg movement among his executives?

Years later, as he sat in his new office and pondered his future, Ben could only smile wryly and remind himself that it was impossible to undo the judgments of the past or to try to counter one's instincts. He was simply most effective at the top; he understood most and catered best to the people up there, perhaps because he was one of them. He knew that it may have been a fault of his—he left himself wide open because of it—but it was the way he was and would continue to be.

There was another habit he had to examine. Oddly enough, it was something of a reverse principle of his preferring to work only at the top. It involved his penchant for taking on too many clients, some of them questionable ones, not so much because he was so hungry to "grow" his business, but also because he was curious about so many people. It had occasionally gotten him into trouble.

He recalled, for example, the fracas in the late 1940s with William O'Dwyer, the crusty mayor of New York City.

A client of Ben's, a businessman and socialite, had mounted a heavy campaign of criticism against O'Dwyer, culminating Martin Luther–style in his nailing a list of complaints to the door of City Hall. The critic was, ironically, the grandson of a close associate of "Boss" William Marcy Tweed, the controversial head of Tammany Hall in the latter half of the nineteenth century. Strange as it seemed, the descendant was accusing O'Dwyer of many of the same charges hurled against Boss Tweed and his own grandfather—corruption, dipping into the city's till, bribing judges. The press promptly seized upon the juicy plum, especially the irony transcending the years. O'Dwyer became furious, and knowing that Ben represented the businessman-critic, charged publicly that "Sonnenberg was the instrument of public relations who had engineered the attack."

Sonnenberg was greatly disturbed by the attack. He knew that he was great at handling the problems of others, but, conversely, that he was very insecure about himself. He knew it and his friends knew it. He would shy away from the slightest personal attack. He didn't want publicity for himself, at least not in those days, much as he wanted it for the people who paid him for it. Yet he was inordinately confident about telling clients how and what to do when they were under attack.

Through a friend, he was advised to contact Theodore Kheel, an attorney and the mayor's labor adviser. Kheel was invited to 19 Gramercy Park and was, Ben saw, suitably impressed. They talked about other things first, and finally Sonnenberg said, "You know, I'm not involved in the attack on the mayor. It's true that I handle public relations for the man who is carrying it on, but this is his frolic, not mine. I am certainly not behind the nailing of the charges to the wall. I do not want to be in contention with His Honor. It is not in my interest. Could you straighten it out?"

Kheel had good-naturedly accepted the mission and afterward related the conversation with Ben to O'Dwyer. The lawyer genuinely liked O'Dwyer—a big, strapping, pipe-smoker who had been a brigadier general in the United States Army— and thought he was almost as fascinating a character as Sonnenberg himself.

"General," Kheel said, "I had a meeting the other day with Ben Sonnenberg."

"What did that faker want?"

"Well, to put it succinctly, General, he knows he's on your shit list, and he would like to get off."

"Well, he's on the list all right," said O'Dwyer, "and he's not gonna get off. But you can tell him this. He can go north and I will go south and we will never have anything to do with each other."

Kheel went back to Sonnenberg. "Ben, I talked to the mayor, and I told him that you were on his shit list and that you wanted to get off, and he said you can go north and he'll go south and the two of you will never meet."

"That's wonderful," said Ben. "How much do I owe you?"

"You don't owe me anything. This is not my regular line of work."

"Then I have to give a dinner party in your honor. What movie would you like to see?"

The incident had taught Sonnenberg a lesson, that he would have to exercise greater caution in selecting clients, a lesson that perhaps he hadn't learned as well as he should have. He would have to temper both his zeal to make money and his zeal to meet and probe all kinds of people, especially now that he was entering this new phase in his career where perhaps all the challenges would be more accentuated and more personal. But the O'Dwyer incident had had a positive side, too. He had made a new friend and business colleague in Ted Kheel; it was a relationship that would last for decades.

A third habit that Ben had to reconsider as he entered his new life was his reliance on his own staff of writers and publicity men. It was a serious consideration because he had always maintained a hand's-off relationship with almost everyone on his P.R. staff, and it was the staff who had made almost all the media contacts, written all the releases, and arranged almost all the meetings with clients intended to directly result in articles in the press. Could he, in fact, go it alone?

The answer was implicit in Ben's own makeup. Of course he could go it alone.

As Ted Kheel observed much later, "The new phase in his life was certainly that. He was older, and he really was not reaching to expand. The great value of Sonnenberg was not the great press releases that his staff put out, the material they got, but his ideas, what he would advise people to do. That was the important thing, and that he could do without a staff. He could determine talent, but he couldn't write. He couldn't draw up a press release. He couldn't make a speech. Even so, while he had that staff of twenty or so, he was a one-man band, he was Ben Sonnenberg, for as long as I remember. In that new phase of his career, he still wanted to make money. He loved to make money, and he would cut himself in on everything. He was very aggressive. If he put a deal together, he'd call you up and he'd call someone else up and if it was a deal, you paid Sonnenberg. There was nothing modest about him. But that period became a totally different phase. I think it involved more of what he was best at doing. It was not running a public-relations firm anymore. And I don't think that his public-relations firm by any traditional standards was outstanding. But he was unique and in that final phase it was all him."

That realization, it became apparent, sustained Sonnenberg and allowed him to confront what to most people would be an actual phase of retirement with calmness and even anticipation. Obviously, it would be a much slower sort of existence, it wouldn't have the pressures and the excitement that flowed from them, but it might well have a new type of depth and involvement. It might be either the golden age in his life or his decline.

Yet, he felt the thrill of the challenge, the excitement of the hunt, as he sipped his glass of tea or glanced down at Park Avenue. He was still only sixty-two years old. Was it so unlikely that all that he had done before might not only be a springboard for even greater, even more dazzling things to come?

11

A
FIREPLACE
IN THE
BATHROOM

"**H**e would come in often, mostly before or after lunch, sometimes alone but more often with someone else, like Alistair Cooke or Brooke Astor or an Oxford professor, and sort of swagger around the cases of silver or porcelain, saying, 'This is such-and-such' or 'so-and-so,' as often as not knowing only a little of what he was talking about. But he cut a figure all right, and we loved to see him."

Edward Munves, Sr., the owner of James Robinson, Inc., the famous West Fifty-seventh Street antique silver and jewelry store, added, "Sonnenberg was a customer off and on for thirty-five years. He had very good taste, but everything he bought had to have flair. It had to be vivid, I suppose, like his own personality. . . ."

If his business pace had slowed down, doubtless only for the time being, it offered Sonnenberg a chance to indulge one of his other great loves, collecting. He could spend more time touring the galleries of Fifty-seventh Street, Madison, Lexington, and Third Avenues, with his great Wall Street friend Robert Lehman. And he could take more leisurely, more extended trips to London and the English countryside with his two closest literary friends, Brendan Gill and Alistair Cooke, where they could sit in restaurants, clubs, or inns and observe the moving panorama or do the gallery and auction tour.

For many years, Ben had played something of a game in his house and then picked it up in the galleries. Often he would go through each room to find an open spot on a wall, on the floor between two pieces of furniture, an empty corner, and envision there yet another objet d'art, a statue or bust, a piece of glass, a clock, a piece of Wedgwood, a butler's chair, or another highboy. It didn't matter that some of his guests seemed either amused or appalled that his walls and rooms were literally crowded with objects. But once he determined what particular location was to be filled, he would scour the galleries, antique shops, and auction rooms for an item closest to what he saw in his mind's eye.

As Alistair Cooke put it later in a preface to an auction catalog of the Sonnenberg house, "For over forty years, he roamed through England (mostly) plucking a Sargent or a Sickert here, an Ingres or an Old Master drawing there, combining in his head, with the skill of a jig-saw champion, an Irish hunt table, a Welsh dresser, a Caroline silver tankard, precious china, sets of Chippendale, many exquisite Queen Anne or Georgian chests and settee beds, to bring them home to their proper setting: the 1845 house he bought (typically enough) in the depth of the depression, when millionaires were back at square one."

In the New York gallery world, the Sonnenberg–Robert Lehman duo became a frequent sight. Lehman, the art patron and playboy banker, had great wealth but no great knowledge of art or artifacts. Sonnenberg had relatively limited wealth but a considerable zest for culture. The result was a lot of money chasing a lot of art without any clear guidance. If Lehman's purchases and Sonnenberg's acquisition of the leavings together included many pieces of questionable merit, many other pieces were fine. "Bobby was like a Medici in his rampant collection of art," said a Sonnenberg associate. "And Ben would buy what Bobby rejected, but that today would be pretty good, even superb."

The publicist, of course, served Lehman in more ways than as a companion in the art galleries. Ben helped Bobby shine his "escutcheon," or improve his corporate and personal image, but Lehman also had a high regard for Ben's instincts as a merger expert. Once Lehman asked Ben to come along when the head of another investment banking firm proposed a meeting with Lehman, looking to a possible merger. As the two of them entered their host's imposing limousine, Ben nodded approvingly at the English-type chauffeur who tended to them. Afterward, Ben noticed that the banker's chauffeur doubled as his butler.

Later, when Lehman asked Sonnenberg for his opinion, Ben replied, "Any man of that wealth who is too stingy to have both a chauffeur and a butler is not a suitable partner for you. Forget it, Bobby." And Lehman did.

It was evident that Lehman's belief in Ben's ability to help sustain his shining public stature was most important to the banker. That high reputation might persist even after he was gone, Lehman believed, and there are people who were close to him who believe that it was Sonnenberg who convinced Lehman that there was a clear way to do that. Perhaps that is why Lehman made it a condition of bequeathing his art collection to the Metropolitan Museum of Art in New York that the museum maintain that collection in its own wing after he passed on.

As for Ben himself, his collecting became an avid process, whether it involved his own selection or the leavings of his friends and clients. He adored brass. Was it for its bright durability or for its ability to blend with everything else? But how well does that glittering alloy of copper and zinc enhance the beauty of the manorial, the antiquities, the lush oriental rugs? He thought very well indeed. And so he assembled 464 pieces of brass, from candlesticks to coal buckets, from sconces to samovars. There were so many of these, as well as urns, andirons, tea kettles, salvers, and weights large and small, that it required one person working full time about three months to clean and polish the entire collection.

It was more than pure greed that made him one of the world's most noted collectors of brass. He genuinely enjoyed looking at the pieces. In the library, his favorite room, the collection ranged from early eighteenth century Scottish candleholders to Venetian gondolas to sea horses. In his bedroom—separate from Hilda's—forty pieces of brass faced walls of a midnight hue. In his own bathroom hung a sumptuous brass chandelier.

In terms of sheer impact, however, it was the vast array of oils, drawings, and prints that almost bowled over first-time visitors to 19 Gramercy Park. Ben started the collection as far back as his first visits in 1922 and 1923 to London and Paris as a field worker to assist in the American relief effort for war-torn Europe. The English historian J. H. Plumb, warden of Christ College, Cambridge, whom silver auctioneer Edward Munves, Sr., remembers sometimes dropping into his store with Sonnenberg, related that the publicist had actually begun his earliest collecting as an American visitor who found himself for the first time with "earnings in his pocket." But, according to Professor Plumb, Sonnenberg's collecting of paintings grew in taste and frequency directly as a result of the companionship of Robert Lehman. Together, they would comb the showrooms of the London dealers, both buying according to their very different incomes. Lehman would pay large sums for the oils, which made up the bulk of the collection. Sonnenberg would necessarily favor less expensive drawings and the efforts of contemporary or not so well-known artists.

Sonnenberg preferred portraits, more of the informal than ancestral variety, rather than landscapes, scenes with more than one figure or still lifes. Some said that was natural since he was so often surrounded by people. But he liked the ornate portrait, too. One of the most striking paintings in the mansion hung in the grand stairway; it was a huge, magnificent portrait of Millicent Hawes, the Duchess of Sutherland, by John Singer Sargent, the American painter. It was so massive and the figure so regal that it captured eyes almost from any floor that looked out on the stairway. The duchess, who gazed imperiously out at the guests, her bared white shoulders and deep cleavage daring anyone to return her gaze, was surrounded by six smaller portraits, all vividly set off by two crystal chandeliers, one on top of the other. Even with the duchess as the centerpiece of his collection of art, however,

Sonnenberg's main interest was expressed in smaller-scale, more intimate drawings, less imposing in their intent. As a result, he was most attracted to such painters as Mary Cassatt, William Merritt Chase, Max Beerbohm, George Luks, Walter Richard Sickert, Augustus John, Giovanni Boldini, Theodore Chasseriau, and Jean Auguste Dominique Ingres.

He acquired some interesting sculptures, too. They ranged from Egyptian reliefs and limestone figures to busts of Gertrude Stein and Marsden Hartley by Jacques Lipchitz. A particular favorite was Jacob Epstein's bronze portrait of W. Somerset Maugham, a friend of Sonnenberg's and a frequent guest. Sonnenberg was intrigued by Epstein's skill in capturing the writer's long-nosed, sunken-cheeked austerity.

The largest part of his overall collection was the eighteenth-century furniture. As a young man who had started out with nothing, it could be reasoned that a prime goal was to acquire much—and what could be more substantial than antique furniture? His flair was evident in his selection, some of his pieces of furniture drawing expressions of amazement and envy from first-time observers. One, for example, was a huge William IV bookcase, which measured twelve feet wide by nine feet high. Two others were a William IV gilt-metal, mounted ebony-inlaid mahogany sideboard, which was eighty-six and a half inches wide and forty-one inches high, and a George I–style burr walnut cabinet, forty-nine and a half inches wide and eighty-nine and a half inches high. Another piece that impressed guests was an early eighteenth-century, carved, walnut, folding library writing table, proud and gleaming in its age.

Brooke Astor, the widow of Vincent Astor, the scion of John Jacob Astor, who was America's richest man when he died in 1848, knew Sonnenberg in the 1950s but avoided his parties. "He was a promoter and I stayed away," she said. But in the late 1960s, they became friends. She attended his dinners and was bowled over by the house and its staff service. "It was the best-run house I've ever been in. He had helped Dorothy Draper, the talented decorator and she did his house with much skill. He so enjoyed the fun of having people in. He had wonderful silver and crystal. And we were all intrigued that he had a servant for every room," she said.

Over a period of thirty or forty years Ben accumulated

enough treasures for any and every taste, provided it was an English taste. But he denied many times that two of his main criteria were quantity and visual impact, a pandering to effect for its own sake. "Of course not," he would respond. "There's nothing deliberate in it. I attire my house to suit myself. But if it also pleases you . . ."

Across the entry hall two dining rooms faced one another. One was a large, formal room, the other was a small, oak-paneled parlor. The big room was standard Victorian, the smaller one crowded with old oak pieces, books, a mantle-piece heavily laden with brass. But the room was so exquisitely "attired" that more than a few guests hated to leave it for the more imposing rooms. Perhaps what stirred them was how Ben and Hilda had arranged a room that was both city-urbane and country-relaxed. It was, incidentally, one of Hilda's favorites of all the thirty-seven rooms.

And then there was the great central staircase—a room in itself, an attention-getter of no mean pretensions. Leading to four of the five floors, a heavy, white wrought-iron balustrade provided both continuity and safety, circling around and around. Paintings and prints and brass and silver on the walls of each landing or in various cases, dominated by the huge Sargent painting and the two chandeliers, completed the dazzling effect.

On the second floor was the William and Mary Room, perhaps the one room that everyone went away remembering. It not only had the best furniture of all the rooms but had actual seventeenth-century carving from a famous, old English mansion, Corinthian columns, and other imported paneling. Many who came were prepared to be impressed at the furnishings: a pair of George I gilt-gesso mirrors circa 1720; a pair of George II carved mahogany window seats; a Queen Anne writing table circa 1710. As for the carvings, there was some documentation that they were really the famous Grinling Gibbons carvings installed in 1670, rather than 1720, in the Cassiobury in Hertfordshire.

Did those who sipped brandy in the William and Mary Room find themselves stirred more by the 1590 painting of Sir Thomas Crompton or by being able to stare at themselves in the superb pair of mirrors in their gilt-gesso frames for which English antique collectors have been known to lose their usual decorum? In either case, the total effect was extraordinary.

Across the second-floor landing was what some considered the finest of bathrooms in a house of nine fine bathrooms. It had a green carpet, a miniscule, mirrored vestibule crammed with silver pieces, a large porcelain washstand with fixtures of nickel, a shower with an enclosure covered in a Chinese wallpaper—and a fireplace.

The second-floor landing was more ornate than some of the actual rooms themselves. What can it possibly offer, sandwiched between the William and Mary Room and the magnificent central stairway? The landing's pièce de résistance was an 1800 Regency wine table, flanked by two handsome armchairs, which opened, if they were ever needed for such a purpose, into couches. Facing these on the walls were some of Sonnenberg's most valued art: a Seurat, a van Gogh, an Ingres, a Degas, and a Vuillard. And accenting all these treasures were chandeliers, candelabras, decanters, and candlesticks. It was only a landing, but one with the riches of a small museum.

On the third floor, Hilda had her own suite and Ben had his bedroom and his library. All had individual pieces of distinction and the overall, mixed-up panache that made the rooms so inviting. One was piqued first to laughter and then to wonder. Why did the Sonnenbergs use objects intended for one purpose for another? Hilda, for example, had an eighteenth-century winecooler in her bedroom which she used as a coffee table. Ben had a pair of French glass blocks Hilda found for him, which he used as ashtrays. And what was the point of a 1772 Torricelian barometer in the library? Why all the books and newspapers scattered about the room in seeming disregard to the orderliness of all the stacked, bound volumes? What was the point of it all? Nothing, perhaps, except that they wanted their home to look like an opened, jumbled treasure chest. After all, where there's a whim, there ought to be a way.

On the fourth floor, the rooms were more utilitarian than the others, with simpler bedrooms and studies. But the fifth floor was another matter, for it contained the largest of all the rooms, Sonnenberg's famous projection room, where he could easily accommodate fifty people. It was filled with couches, armchairs, divans—all, surprisingly, covered with chintz, somewhat too prosaic for the host but the hostess liked it. Most could be swiveled around so one could face the screen. Of course, there was the handsome, white marble fireplace mantel, the Sargent and Nadelman artworks, and that overwhelming William IV bookcase, not to mention the full concert grand, facing three imposing busts on a picture window that looked down on the private park. The sheer size, the sumptuousness of that projection room was awesome. It was only right and logical that the room was at the top of the house, where advance movie releases, fine roast beef sandwiches, and a fine choice of drinks served by white-gloved retainers topped off an otherwise fine evening. All planned that way? No, of course not—but no one believes such smooth modesty.

In case one was not quite impressed enough by the projection room, immediately outside it was an oval-shaped landing where Sonnenberg had posted his autograph collection, all at eye level, of course. It included the autographs of Enrico Caruso, Rudyard Kipling, Somerset Maugham, and Claude Debussy.

As Alistair Cooke related, "Not long ago, two of Queen Elizabeth's equerries stayed the night there. They were ravished by the uniform style and grandeur of the place, by the absence of any seedy nook or cranny. 'Buckingham Palace,' one of them said, 'was never like this.' "

And Louis Calta reported in the *New York Times* on November 15, 1967, when he wrote about Sonnenberg's opening-night party in his home for the play *The Promise* by Aleksei Arbuzov, that Valentin M. Kamenev, cultural consul of the Soviet embassy in Washington, observed, "This is a museum. They should have a guide. There are some excellent drawings and paintings."

But, as Ben Sonnenberg, Jr., related in the *Nation* in describing the reaction of a famous playwright to the ultimate Sonnenberg bathroom, "Tennessee Williams was heard to say, 'It looked so shabby when I took it out, I couldn't go.' "

"My parents conspired well in the house. They lived there for forty-eight years. My father had a compulsion to buy, my mother to decorate. Together they made a fetish of antique furniture."

Ben's son, Ben, Jr., wasn't happy at 19 Gramercy Park South. He wrote about it at length in 1982 in *Grand Street*, a literary magazine for which he was co-editor. A poet, playwright, and essayist, he displayed traits of all three inclinations in a long, bittersweet, rambling recollection.

At first, they collected like children, to renew the world. Later, with money, acquiring things was very far from naive. The justifications! the reasons! Good business was one. Well might it have been. Still, like all of the genus Collectors' Child, while I was jealous principally of my parents' unstinted passion, I hated worse their profession of a practical purpose. And why? Their passion suggested only that I was subordinate to Sheraton, second to George the Second, and not so much fun as a cheerful chintz: which a seven-year-old would of course resent but could nevertheless comprehend. But their tacit profession that all was not in fact what it so clearly seemed: that to me was trumped! arrant make-believe! typical of adults! . . .

My father bought art and bought art and bought art. He and my mother appeared most at one placing this "amusing scrap" or shifting that "little piece."

Not only did art dealers minister to this otherwise troubled union, they had also noticed me as at least an important object. I repaid the favor, trying to be as much like them as I could. I copied their accents, wore tweed caps and smoked Le Khédive cigarettes. Could such a life be mine? "And to think," I might say, in the late afternoons, over the drawings by Constantin Guys, the engravings by Felicien Rops, to some young woman bemused by my ritual delay, "there are men who'd show a young girl *this* . . . and *this* . . ." Only twenty and already big with brokers, agents and props! (Or, twenty and still posing! Significant both of having grown up with ceremony and servants, and of a sadism that can be truly practiced only by liars.) . . ."

Earlier, Ben, Jr., wrote in the article,

Looked at from the street, my house was not much: large, but just to the standard of wealthy pre–Civil War

New York, more "Murray Hill" than "Washington Square," and too sheerly ample for good design. Except for being a corner building (at 20th Street and Irving Place), it belonged to that bland type of mansion, plentiful in New York, which always is being converted from misuse or dilapidation into monuments to individualism understood as earning-a-fortune. . . . Nineteen Gramercy Park was quaint, self-conscious, a "mad" expense. But its finally heroic shape was due to its being in town: that is what made it conspicuous and expressive as an excess. A similar effort in Greenwich, Connecticut, would have had different results.

Room after comfortable, colorful room: various, orderly, studied, profuse; devoted to what Henry James defined "the mysteries of ministration to rare pieces"; all brought together, and made to cohere: through force of furnishing, so to speak: in a sumptuous, costly, luxurious style known once as Capuan. It made a unique impression. Not, as with Frick and the subtle Duveen, of a wedding of riches to expert taste, but of something much more peculiar. In "Louis Philippe, or the Interior," [Walter] Benjamin says: "For the private individual the private environment represents the universe. In it he gathers remote places and the past. His drawing room is a box in the world theater." And the verb that follows will nail the point. My home gripped the imagination as wholly a fiction, a play, a dream: formal and yet almost overcharged with personal emblems and feelings. . . .

All was phantasmagoric. To me, at least, the house stood for taste and culture in an era of mass fright: quite as if these were enough armament, together with making money. For it to succeed, it had to exclude. And with exceptional force. Decoration was in, but poetry and music had no place. Talk of people was in, but not of ideas; of Democratic electioneering, but not of politics. Biographies, table talk, memoirs, "characters" crowded the shelves; portraits and "conversations" were everywhere on the walls.

It was more a venue for parties than ever an actual home. Like the Dedlock mansion in Bleak House,

"Fairyland to visit, but a desert to live in." If a home, however, then Heartbreak House, so far as Shaw's play does indeed represent "leisured, cultured Europe" before the First World War. Only, alas, by the time I was nine, *two* world wars had occurred, and my mother and father had lived through both. . . .

My father was an impressive man in the mode of the late nineteenth century: a "new" man to the dons and peers he loved to entertain, an "aristocrat" to the company heads he was hired by. His snobbism was the same as Morel's in *Le Temps retrouvé*, Proust having observed "with the infallibility of one himself susceptible," in Theodor Adorno's words, "that Anglomania and the cult of stylized living are found less among aristocrats than among those aspiring to rise." It led to peculiar locutions ("My man will show you out") as well as to the fairyland air of 19 Gramercy Park. . . . Secrecy lay at the very core of my father's power at home. In addition, mystification was a genuine part of his work. He also justified earning by incantatory allusions to a fabulous boyhood (it seemed so to me) with actual deprivations: to growing up "an immigrant boy," as he liked to exult, "in a tenement-house on the Lower East Side" where the plumbing was out in the hall.

On the other hand, justification itself was called for by no one but him. He pointed thereby to a pre-bourgeois past that, to quote Adorno again, "survives in the shame felt at being paid for personal services and favors." The pre-bourgeois world, involving pogroms with dreams of consoling wealth, though frankly a legend, was used nonetheless to explain why he'd had to earn money in amounts as large as "they" would allow for as long as "they" would allow it. . . . The shame had a meaning besides. His business was public relations. Our house was a blush for this fact. Not only in looking established, while public relations was deemed "fly-by-night," as he himself often remarked. But in being so brazenly stagy. This argued no real difference between the public and the private. Indeed, when my father was showing off, there *was* nowhere private at home. What things had cost was a part of his spiel as he took strangers through the house. No one corner was different from the rest of the house in taste. The "style of the whole" was in cupboards and drawers as well as in every room.

Also staginess made an embarrassment of the truthful and ideal. I reacted the more against sound common sense. All was a shibboleth. "You'll have to earn your own living some day." What sort of fool did he think I was? In this respect, I'm inclined to believe, the house was no less a frustration to him than a riddle to me.

All this would not have been surprising to Ben, Sr. Actually, his son had written several articles with similar sentiments for *The Nation* some years earlier to the father's embarrassment. But Ben had shrugged it off. Ben, Jr., was that way, "an arrogant young man who sometimes was very naive," the father told his friends. Not very appreciative of what his parents had done for him, an idealist with literary pretensions. Was it all so surprising? Friends of the family debated the matter, some arguing that it was unusual all right, considering how successful the father was, others retorting that that was just why they weren't getting along. But all agreed that it was unfortunate but maybe not very significant.

Certainly the father did not allow the filial criticism in any way to curb his buying and collecting.

"I might not see him for a month or six weeks but he would always come in after an interval like that," said Edward Munves, Sr. "My first impression of him was that here was a strange, little man, with that square derby, the high-cut, four-button jacket, who just 'wanted to look around.' But after a couple of visits, we were 'Ed' and 'Ben.' He was an easy guy to get to know. And a great name-dropper. 'I am having lunch once I leave here with so-and-so,' he would say, 'or I've just had lunch with so-and-so.' "

Sonnenberg's quest in his selection was always for something different, "vivid." First, he bought reproductions, especially servers of all sorts, platters and trays, then old glass, old porcelain, old silver at the James Robinson store. The "flair" he sought meant not just a decanter, but one of unusual size; not just a piece of porcelain, but one that had

BOOK THREE

bright, arresting colors and design. Each piece had to be an attention-getter.

Invited to dinner at 19 Gramercy Park, Munves found himself intrigued by the mixture of people, mostly from society or the arts. There were never more than eight or ten present and the service was "beautiful," Sonnenberg behaving more "like an Englishman than an American." Mostly at such times, he was restrained, not holding forth but circulating from one room to another after dinner wherever two or three people had wandered.

The walls of the Sonnenberg home were covered with a silk material, and fresh flowers were placed throughout all the rooms, Munves recalls. Ben was "proud of showing his possessions. Hilda took great interest in the colors and decor, creating the background for the things that Ben purchased."

Sonnenberg's zest for flair didn't always work, however. When the Robinson Store moved to the south side of East Fifty-seventh Street, Munves asked Ben to look over the site, its surroundings, and suggest some means of dramatizing the store's move. Sonnenberg offered a startling recommendation. Shaking his head at what he saw, Ben said, "You'll never get much attention with this sort of quiet background. What you must do when you open the new store is have a dozen beautiful models holding bottles of champagne and pouring it for all the guests."

Munves, however, did not accept the suggestion. "We weren't that sort of store and we opened more modestly," he said. "But that was Ben. Everything had to have flair."

12

ACCOMMODATOR, SENIOR GRADE

In his final phase, Ben Sonnenberg truly worked alone. He was still very active, but on a smaller scale. There was no sadness in him, none, at least, that he would allow anyone to see. And in fact the last decade and a half were, in some ways, the best years of his life and career.

From the mid-1960s onward, Sonnenberg was his own man. He stopped giving his big parties, limited the smaller ones, and phased out his beloved practice of showing the latest movies to his guests before the public saw them. In fact, he even gave up his limousine and chauffeur. When a friend asked him how long he could go on without something that he had obviously enjoyed for so long, he replied, "Listen, I find now that I have three hundred chauffeurs. I just go out on the street and I lift my index finger. It's absolutely great. I use taxis everywhere, except when I go to the airport or for a trip to Princeton or someplace like that, when I hire a Cadillac and chauffeur. I am free, even in my choice of transportation."

Those who were close to him recollect fleeting glimpses of a new, recharged Ben in those first years of his independence. On a trip to a client who had a sizable but remotely located business in rural, upstate New York, Sonnenberg sauntered up Main Street in his Chesterfield, homburg, spats, and cane, returning the open-mouthed stare of local burghers and tobacco-chompers with a haughty grin. "He was like a shark in a tank of guppies that day," said a friend who had accompanied him. "The bloody ripples must have lasted for weeks." At the annual Inner Circle dinner, the year's big opportunity for the New York political writers to rub elbows with the politicians from New York, Albany, and Washington, Sonnenberg would walk into the grand ballroom of the hotel in which it was being held, a bit late of course, and hands would reach up from one table after another to grasp his. Men who hadn't seen him for a week, a month, or a year would rise to pound his back, bandy one-liners, and kid him about some coup he had pulled off years earlier. His normally sallow cheeks would turn pinker and pinker. Often he would take a young protégé or two with him to luncheons and dinners for big givers to liberal, Democratic, or Jewish causes. Obviously, he wanted to show them that there was a giving as well as a taking side to his life and hoped that, if they were to emulate him, such experiences might mold them.

He became a close associate and adviser to Richard Salomon, the chairman of the Charles of the Ritz cosmetics company and a philanthropist and fund raiser, to help him get the wealthy to pledge to various philanthropic drives. Asked years later for some reminiscences of that relationship, Salomon, normally very outgoing, demurred. "I'd rather not," he said. "Ben had ways of helping us attract funds that were clever, possibly controversial. I'd rather not get into it."

One of Sonnenberg's most gratifying new activities revealed him to be a very humane man, not merely a professional. It had begun earlier when he still had the agency. A client who headed a large company that Sonnenberg represented was divorcing his wife, and he was nervous about the publicity that the rift would create. On Ben's advice, one of his own most trusted staff members accompanied the client to Reno, where divorces could still be obtained simply and even amicably, to ensure that the family breakup involving a well-known businessman didn't receive ugly media coverage. The results were ideal. Nothing appeared anywhere, either in Reno or New York. It was all kept friendly, very low key—and quiet.

The more compassionate activities of Ben's new life were quite different, even more wholesome, than his previous approach to clients. He began counseling wealthy widows who seemed at loose ends in their lives because of loneliness and the loss of husbands, who in most cases had dominated the family. They often thought that the wealth they had inherited might somehow be put to better use. As Jim Bowling of Philip Morris related, "Most of these women didn't know what to do with their lives. Ben would counsel them what charities they should identify with, how to lead a more active life, and how to become useful people. It's not a common, everyday problem that most of us would ever know about. But it was a growing thing, especially with women outliving men. Coping with their lives as wealthy widows of middle or advanced age had become a whale of a problem. I remember a number of cases in which there were widows who had not been very active during their husbands' lives. The men had been very busy making fortunes. The women inherited the money, and not so many of them knew what to do with it or with their lives.

"Ben would get fees of twenty-five, even fifty thousand dollars to help them," Bowling said. "He was such an arbiter of the social scene that he could provide a strange, unknown but actually very useful service. He would take a lady who had never had a social or public role beyond her husband and her family life, who suddenly was left alone in her later years with a massive amount of money and was facing a very dull, meaningless life. And for a fee Ben would bring them into the world. He would get such requests, assignments, mostly by recommendation, by word of mouth, just as he did publicity-counseling assignments. He became known for being particularly good at that sort of thing. And for the ladies it was an enormous bargain. There they were sitting around with all this money, and Ben would tell them, 'You know, there's something you should become involved in,' and proceed to find out what their interests were, and he would put them into the right place. They became active in some useful cause, and he would help them to contribute to things that were good for society and therefore gave them a real lease on life, which most of them had never had. It made them become personalities in their own right."

That sort of sideline enterprise, however, didn't deter Sonnenberg from pushing ahead with his effort to cement and expand his corporate publicity consultant's activity. More than ever before, since he had clearly avoided the routine press-agentry side of the public-relations business, this meant working harder to get to the very top of the big corporations. The one-to-one relationship with the chairman, president, and chief executive was what he savored most anyway; it was the field that he had plowed more effectively than the head of any other P.R. agency, and now it was to be his lifeline. But, in the process of furthering such relationships, Sonnenberg became a thorn in the side of younger agency heads on the way up.

In one such case, the young, eager-eyed head of a growing public-relations agency, found himself being invited to lunch at The Colony or Le Cote Basque by Sonnenberg. It was all friendly enough and quite flattering to the younger man.

"He was very nice to me and I listened to these attempts at flattery and I was, of course, very respectful," the agency man recalled. "I remember once when he invited me to The Colony, sitting next to me was Helena Rubinstein with that white parchment face and the jet-black hair in her eighties. I'll never forget that. I was still quite a young man, and I certainly remembered that when I was in college the two most famous public-relations men in the U.S. were Ben Sonnenberg and Edward Bernays. And here I was, being courted by the famous Ben Sonnenberg."

Ben insisted that the most effective way to operate was with "the top people; you don't deal with the technicians and the workers."

As the younger man recalls it, he told Ben, "Look, please don't tell me that, if you know the publisher or the editor-in-chief of the *New York Times* or the *Wall Street Journal*, you are going to force a story in because of that contact."

"Now, young man, you listen," said Ben. "There's a good deal more to it than that."

"Oh, I know that under certain circumstances if you get into trouble," said the agency head, "you can get someone to stop things for you. You can encourage someone to look into things for you. But you really can't make things happen just by knowing someone at the top."

"If you know the people," insisted Sonnenberg, "you *can* guide some things along. I've had a couple of experiences where I found out something that was going to happen in the *Wall Street Journal* and *Time* magazine and that gave me knowledge, and knowledge, young man, *is* power. I found out what was going to happen from the medium—at the top. I then called the head of the company that was the subject or target of the article and told him, 'Say, you know, I was over at *Time* magazine or the *Wall Street Journal* and learned that an article was forthcoming on your company. It will please you to know that I was able to discuss in some depth the matter in a positive way. You might want to get next Monday's issue and see the results of what might otherwise have been . . .' You see, young man," Sonnenberg told the younger man, "that's why it pays to work at the top and go to the top. You would be surprised how many times, simply by knowing it was going to happen from the top, I could give the impression to the top that I had done it or helped do it."

The agency chief recalls that he kept looking at Sonnenberg after the older man had finished, thinking, This is a self-demeaning thing he is saying to me. He was announcing that he had deceived businessmen into thinking that he had done something for them by using knowledge that he had obtained from other businessmen.

"Now I understand that, with the advantage of a decade and a half's hindsight," the agency head said. "But to describe it to me then as an achievement was very odd. I don't think that that type of operator, however brilliant and famous he is, can operate in the market these days in that way. I don't know if people are more perceptive or have a different sense of ethics in the public-relations field. But I do think that there is a professionalism today that can function well without having to do that kind of thing. Ben did tell me some stories in which he had a very important business influence, but he might have been showing off. I'm sure that much of it was true, but some of what he told me was self-serving or convenient anecdotage.

The gist of it all was that it was a tricky situation that could be damaging to companies, and he had been able to blunt that damage. Afterward, he gave the companies involved very wise counsel about what to do and what not to do and what to say or not to say. As I recall they made a lot of sense.

"What I came away with," he went on, "was that he may have embellished the incidents, and maybe certain elements of them were accidental, and other people may have helped—but there was too much of it and too much intricate detail to be false. He was obviously a very wise man, who had a good, detached vision of what you could do and what you couldn't. He was just a terrific strategist. Granted, I was getting the evidence from him. But his strategic sense and the way he described his recommendations and what ensued—it was very, very impressive."

As their meetings continued, Sonnenberg told him, "Young man, I and people like me are accommodators. Yes, accommodators. We provide a companion service to advertising, but we add something else: wise judgment. We develop good instincts and psychology, and we get people together. By that, I mean many businessmen make a lot of money, say, out in the Midwest, but they become rather hungry to know and meet their peers and to know beautiful women who may be famous in the New York theater and to jaw with congressmen and others in Washington. Well, we accommodate them. Then, young man, you see, there's the other side. There are those congressmen, senators, other businessmen, and those beautiful women who want to meet the big businessmen from Chicago, Detroit, and Denver. Getting people together, making the right mix, works very well indeed. The people who are private get excited about meeting the people who are public, and the people who are public enjoy parading before those who are private. And there we are, the accommodators."

Sonnenberg was still having some parties at the house, and he invited the young agency chief to one. It was a big affair, with almost two hundred guests, and the hubbub was constant, exciting. An Indian pianist played that night, and the guest remembered that Norman Mailer was there. "Ben and Norman seemed to know each other well. Ben seemed, in fact, to know everyone well," he said.

As Sonnenberg pursued him, with "at least four luncheons and long talks about all kinds of things," it became apparent to the much younger public relations man—he was about thirty-eight to Sonnenberg's early sixties—that Ben had a very clear goal in all this.

"I think he was building me to a sense of rapport with him, a feeling of being mutually comfortable," the agency head said. "He was telling me that he respected me, and he was finding ways in which I was similar to him in this period that would make me viable or effective in the field. But he said that regardless of the kind of work you do, your staff does, candidly, that's for technicians; it's more like a sort of advertising. I don't mean to deprecate it—by no means—but I think you should get into this other world I am talking about and I can help you."

Recalling the particular conversation, he said that Sonnenberg repeated, "Yes, you ought to get into it more and more. It certainly helped me."

"I'm not so sure I have an interest in it," the other man countered.

"Well, you can't make the real money and get to a level of real power and involvement unless you do."

"I'm doing fine, Ben. I enjoy my work."

"Why don't you mull it over?"

"Of course."

On another occasion, when Sonnenberg visited the busy offices of the other's agency, he stared curiously around at the active office traffic, the young men and young women dashing by, the shrill cacophony of telephones ringing. As they went out to lunch, Ben asked, "How many people do you have on that floor?"

"Oh, about thirty-five or forty."

"My God, what do they all do? How do you train them? How smart can they be?"

Painstakingly, the agency chief explained the process of marketing public relations, hiring and developing people who could obtain media coverage of products and services as an adjunct to advertising. By the time he was done, Sonnenberg was shaking his head ruefully. "I've had my agency, and even then I couldn't delegate counsel. Today, I'm on my own, but occasionally I have one or two technicians," Ben said. "I need them to grind out a release when that's necessary. But I can't delegate who I am or what I do. It's a personal service that I provide. You can't build it into other people."

He paused and added, "I don't know what you're building, young man. You obviously can do the kind of thing that you do and do it well. But you're equipped to do the kind of thing that I do, too, and you should. You would have more fun and you would have a larger platform, but instead it seems to me you are getting bogged down in routine matters."

"Ben, let me explain something," the other man said. "This is what is happening in the field I am in and that you have been in. It is becoming more professional in the way of communications services that corporations obviously need and want. In addition to their internal staffs, they need all sorts of specialists, additional counsel, and outside, detached viewpoints. Some of these come from people with professional journalistic backgrounds who can help them in their communications with the media and give them counsel growing out of multifarious experiences with other industries. . . ."

Sonnenberg nodded in appreciation. "Yes, there's no doubt about what you say. That's why I am enjoying this new contact of ours. And I would like to continue our relationship on a more formal basis. I've never wanted to build anything quite like you describe, and now, as you know, I have lessened my activity. It's as if the clients are going away because I wanted them to."

Afterward, at lunch, Sonnenberg got down to business. "You know, of course, that I am no longer a consultant for your client, but I understand that you are now their agency for both corporate and product. As you know, I am totally familiar with the company, as well as many others that could use your services. You obviously operate on your level very effectively, but you are not working with people who are on the boards of directors of companies, and you don't deal with presidents or chairmen. They're all somewhat older than you and are accustomed to dealing with a man of their age or older. They look up to him, you see. I could introduce you to all of them and get you involved with them. Just one of them would pay for my annual fee, apart from whatever counsel I could give you. I could do this and more for an annual fee of fifty thousand dollars. It would more than pay for itself."

The agency head took his time answering. "I don't seem to have any trouble getting new business," he said, "and my agency is growing. With all due respect, Ben, I don't see any need to get into that."

Sonnenberg did some more selling and after a while he suggested, "Well, would you consider a fee of twenty-five thousand dollars? That's practically nothing, isn't it?"

Before he replied, the agency man recalls that he was amazed to hear it, considering Sonnenberg's reputed great wealth. "Ben," he said, "it's not really a question of the fee. It's just that I don't see any need to work out that sort of arrangement. I must reluctantly say no."

The older man appeared to take the turndown graciously, and the conversation shifted in a completely different direction. Listening to Sonnenberg's lively if convoluted speech, the younger man felt a few guilt pangs. The famous publicist seemed very powerful and self-confident. It occurred to him that perhaps Sonnenberg actually would have liked the connection with him, but that you can't offer to be a consultant to a younger man without rationalizing it by taking a fee for the services. The point, perhaps, was that you can't want to dabble in another man's career just to keep busy. The fee—especially in view of Sonnenberg's affluence—was merely to formalize it. Or was it?

Afterward, they would see each other in restaurants and Ben would be affable. But their socializing had ended.

William Ruder, who with David Finn had founded Ruder & Finn, one of New York's most successful public-relations agencies, had something of a similar experience with Sonnenberg. Ruder & Finn had succeeded the Sonnenberg Agency as the agency at Philip Morris. Ruder & Finn had also hired Frank Saunders away from the Sonnenberg Agency before it became just Ben himself. There were no hard feelings about it between Sonnenberg and Ruder. One reason may have been that they had a common friend in George Weissman. George and Bill Ruder had worked together for Sam Goldwyn's studio in Hollywood. George joined Sonnenberg's agency, Ruder opened his own P.R. firm, and they remained friends. During the early 1960s, George phoned Bill and told him that Ben Sonnenberg would like to meet him. The same message came to Ruder from Jim Bowling, the Philip Morris communications executive, who told him, "You should meet Ben Sonnenberg. He's going to stay on as our consultant."

Ruder did not take the initiative, but one day his phone rang and he heard a mellifluous voice say, "This is Ben Sonnenberg. Everyone says we should meet. So come over to my house. I'll be delighted to see you."

A time was arranged, and Bill Ruder appeared. From the moment he entered, he realized that the house had been organized to be as "awesome as possible." An easygoing type, Ruder would have liked to linger and study the walls and landing, but Leonard Horn, the butler, moved along briskly. Upstairs, in the library, Ruder met Sonnenberg. Ruder found his host as "awesome as possible." Ben was dressed in a purple smoking jacket over a dark vest with a gold chain, a pale ascot at his throat, and he was sitting on a sofa, drinking tea from a huge glass.

Ben gestured to a chair, ordered the butler to get Ruder a drink, and kept smiling genially at his guest. Finally, he said, "I've been following Ruder & Finn for some years now, and it pleases me to see two nice young men like you two making a go of it."

"Thank you," said Bill.

"It is reassuring to see the business renewing and sustaining itself under two men like you and Dave Finn."

"Thanks again."

"Reassuring it is."

He sipped the tea and studied Bill Ruder. Then Ben sighed and put his glass down. "As for me," he observed, "I prefer no longer to be active in the communications business, certainly much less than I was. I have had a long run at it."

Some small talk ensued and after a while Sonnenberg said, "You know, I would be happy to be considered a sponsor of Ruder & Finn and its young entrepreneurs. So many things pass my line of vision. I could recommend business to you for a consideration. Tell me about your clients."

Ruder listed them with a brief description of their publicity needs, and Ben kept nodding with each one. "Fine, just fine," he repeated with each one. Then Sonnenberg told his guest about some of the clients he had had, some of whom he still represented as an adviser, the names and the companies they headed reeling off much like a "Who's Who" of American business.

Graciously, Bill said, "That's very impressive, Ben. You paved the way for younger men like me to see a direction."

"It's very kind of you to say that," Ben told him. "I'd like to see you again."

As Bill left, he couldn't help feeling that he had been somehow manipulated. Patronizing Ruder may have been Sonnenberg's only mistake. Maybe it was a normal reaction, Ruder thought, for a successful man twenty years older than another successful man to "seem superior while being friendly, or to deal with his ego while laying the groundwork for transacting business with the other." But the meeting had been all too structured, Ruder concluded, and he walked away uncomfortably, with a sense of Sonnenberg having hoisted "a monkey on my back" by his final comment:

"We have a common goal, I'm sure, don't we, Bill? Let's get together again. I'll await your call."

Ruder did not call. He knew that he wouldn't be invited by Ben to one of his social events because he wasn't important enough to be "in that cultural circle." But Sonnenberg did call, only it was to make a different sort of invitation. "There is a client I want to recommend you to," he said. "Do you know Monte Shapiro of General Instrument Corporation? No? Well, I have recommended you to him. But I think we should meet first, don't you?"

They met briefly. Ben didn't mention a finder's fee again. Ruder & Finn had a policy against it, but Bill Ruder didn't refer to it as he hadn't at their first meeting. However, Bill found himself observing, "If this works out with General Instrument and I feel a business arrangement with you was appropriate, I will contact you."

"Yes, I wish you would," said Ben. "I would like to be part of it as a sort of consultant."

"Well, I don't know if that would work," Bill said. "But we'll see."

When Monte Shapiro and Bill Ruder met, they hit it off well, but the businessman never mentioned Sonnenberg.

Afterward, Ruder wrote to Ben and thanked him for the recommendation. They did not see each other again.

Oddly enough, despite the fact that Sonnenberg never did
get together with them on a professional basis, younger prac-
titioners such as Gershon Kekst, Herbert Rowland and Bill
Ruder had only the most enthusiastic regard for him as a professional practitioner and as a human being. "The thing that
was so impressive to me about him were his great qualities of
perception, shrewdness, insight, and grace," Rowland said.
"He influenced many people in the public-relations business by
his example and philosophy. And as an alchemist and host, an
alchemist of people, he was extremely graceful, in his manner
of transition in conversation. I know he had little formal educa-
tion, but he came across as a very cultured guy, a cultivated
guy however he came by it."

Bill Ruder saw Sonnenberg as a "superb publicity man.
A very shrewd, smart man who had a finely tuned instinct for
the public mind. There were businessmen who lusted after
Ben, wanted to become a client of his so that they could wear
it as a sort of merit badge."

These are strange comments from professionals whom
Sonnenberg had courted for business reasons, and unsuccess-
fully at that. But that was the effect he had on many people,
an indelible charm even if it concealed an incredible opportunist, a consummate accommodator.

Irving Straus didn't heed Ben's advice but, after the fact,
it didn't hurt their mutual cordiality.

In the mid-sixties, Straus was a partner at the Ralph E.
Samuel stock brokerage in New York. Donald C. Samuel, head
of the firm, was much taken with Sonnenberg, especially after
the publicist had managed to obtain a favorable piece for the
company in *Fortune* and had introduced him to a fascinating
mélange of people at 19 Gramercy Park. In 1965, Straus, also
invited there, found it "very old world, genteel amid opulent
surroundings. Ben was winding down those big dinners, but
this one was evidently as lavish as any. He was a fine host. He
brought a very varied group of people together, let them confront one another, and made sure he kept the conversation
going. He had that touch of sparking it and then receding into
the background."

When Straus decided that he wanted to switch careers from being part of a brokerage to operating his own financial public-relations agency, he approached Ben for advice. He was dismayed when Sonnenberg firmly discouraged him.

"It's a twenty-four-hour commitment, Irving," said Ben. "It requires constant thinking and doing. Are you ready for that? In addition, the fees you will get will hardly equate with the work you will need to do, and your real income will necessarily have to come from other sources. In some cases, I can take my fee in stock, and that's why I like to work with some smaller companies. But, by and large, if you get any satisfaction from this business, you will derive it mainly from your own sense of satisfaction from a job well done. Most times, clients won't express gratitude. I've represented General Motors Corporation for some years, but they have never commented on my work. I suppose as long as they keep the checks coming, I am performing satisfactorily. It's a tough business, my friend."

Despite Sonnenberg's warnings, Straus decided that he understood Wall Streeters well enough to help them in their media needs, and he chose to pursue his new career. He told Sonnenberg of his decision. "I would see him afterward in a restaurant or on the street," Straus recalled, "and he would be unfailingly cordial and gallant. He harbored no ill feelings because I hadn't listened to him. Actually, I had listened. He was very persuasive in preparing me for the realities of the business."

Sonnenberg, however, may have met his match in Stanley Marcus, the chairman of Neiman-Marcus, who sold his famous fashion chain in the 1970s and became a consultant. They were two of a kind, showmen and individualists, personalities who made their own way in the world partly by a ceaseless zest, partly by skillful hype. For over forty years, they jested and jousted with each other, throwing off sparks that created a deep, mutual respect.

Their relationship began in the 1930s when Marcus was only twenty-nine, an executive vice-president in the Dallas company started by his father, aunt, and uncle in 1907. The stores were considering venturing into national advertising, and the quest soon led to Sonnenberg, then only in his midthirties. The two ambitious, young men formed a close friendship. Because Ben was a few years older, with a mind and disposition already at least partly matured, he was somewhat paternal with Stanley. As their businesses grew, so did their mutual interests—and their jibing at one another. Once, asking if the publicist had seen a designer that Stanley had introduced him to, Ben told the merchant, "That's the trouble with you. You stick to old friends. You must scrape off the old barnacles and strike out for new faces."

It was, Marcus said later, "one of my first exposures to Sonnenberg's famous cynicism." Responding, he said, "Ben, sometimes I think you like to meet new people and invite them to your home so that you can eventually pull them on a string, like puppets. Aren't you the friendly, local puppeteer?"

Sonnenberg said, "I much prefer to be deemed the accommodator. I try to give people what they want, but in the manner I want to give it to them."

Over the years, there were many dinners and discussions at 19 Gramercy Park and in the best restaurants. Marcus, who never shrank from expressing himself at length, was, however, a good listener; and Sonnenberg realized that his friend, although a merchant, had a solid, instinctive feel for public relations. It became obvious, too, that the publicist liked spouting off, especially to someone who absorbed all of it and put much of it into practice.

"He understood human motivation," Marcus recalled, "and often told me stories about his Wall Street cronies. He regarded most of the financial tycoons as an unscrupulous lot and a lot of them as stuffed shirts. He continued to work for them, but he had no illusions about any of them. He liked to tell stories about how they fought over women and power. Ben knew lots about them, their mistresses and the women that their mistresses didn't know about. But he was very discreet, so far as I knew."

They saw each other well into Sonnenberg's "retirement" period as Marcus frequently moved from Dallas to New York, building new links in Neiman-Marcus's growing chain of stores, cementing ties with the fashion houses of Seventh Avenue.

One night, they had dinner at the Maisonette Russe at the St. Regis Hotel in Manhattan. Ben had arranged to dine there on the Russian New Year's Eve. At midnight, as a highlight, a coterie of White Russian women strode out, bearing a silver tray on which a white rooster teetered. Since it was all for charity, Ben tossed a hundred-dollar bill at the rooster. Laughing, he told Stanley, "That shows I don't keep a grudge. A few decades ago, those people kicked me off the streets of Minsk."

When Marcus occasionally kidded him about his unusual manner of dress, Sonnenberg told him soberly, "If I dressed like you do, people would say, 'Who is that fat, little Jew?' This way, I am distracting, compelling people to ask, 'Who is that fascinating, little man?' "

When he heard some critical observers complain that everything Sonnenberg did was calculated and at its core rooted in a yen to profit from it, Marcus recalled that Ben told him:

"You son-of-a-bitch. You're the only guy who has milked me for forty years and paid me nothing."

Stanley Marcus, in fact, never did pay Sonnenberg a nickel, but he did pay him considerable attention, respect, and affection.

13

SAUNTERING THROUGH THE TWILIGHT

Sonnenberg liked to tell some of his closest friends that he had earned somewhere between $25 million and $30 million in his professional lifetime. It was a staggering sum for "a poor lad from the Lower East Side." Even considering that it was spread over fifty years, since he had started in business as a Broadway press agent, his estimate meant that on an annual basis he had earned between five hundred and six hundred thousand dollars a year. It was more than most corporation chiefs could boast of earning and probably more than any of his clients earned.

In his "retired" state, the final fifteen years of his life, his earnings were considerably less, but he was already so well fixed that it didn't matter. Despite his cutting back on large parties and even surrendering his limousine, the expense of maintaining such a large house and a summer home in Provincetown were high. He managed it, but there were times when he felt the psychological pressure of a reduced income. Hence, his proselytizing of other, younger agency chiefs to accept him as a consultant.

Money, though, wasn't one of his main goals during his later years. He enjoyed his new, relaxed life. He often had breakfast with Senator Abraham Ribicoff of Connecticut, luncheon or dinner with Jim Bowling, Brendan Gill, or Alistair Cooke. He had the unusual pleasure of dealing with fewer clients but on a more personal basis. He enjoyed the social activities, the preparations, the ambience, and the details of service of his "salon," the smaller rooms of his Gramercy Park mansion, where increasingly he invited writers—one, two, or three at a time—to hear them throw literary darts at each other.

More than anything, he enjoyed the opportunity to read, to add to his box of favorite epigrams, to muse over a long, fascinating career, to shop the galleries and auction houses, and to meet with the tycoons and creative people who stimulated him. He enjoyed, in fact, being himself. Retiring from the hurly-burly of agency life at sixty-two years of age, he had spit out the bit in his mouth and was sauntering through the twilight of his life. His family was pleased, very pleased. And some of his older clients, who were still afraid to take the same step, were openly envious and didn't mind saying so.

Ben also had satisfaction from Helen's life. She had married Michael Tucker, a stockbroker whom Ben liked very much, and they had two delightful children, Steven and Barbara, and lived not too far away on Manhattan's Upper East Side. Ben, Jr., who could be a trial but somehow had managed to grab a corner of the old man's heart, had married Wendy Nash, and they also lived in Manhattan with their three daughters, Susanna, Emma, and Saidee. Although his father kept telling friends who inquired about his son's career, "Ben, Jr., is studying to be a gentleman," the son had found his way at least to a certain extent. He had become a poet and book reviewer who published in magazines such as *The Nation*, a playwright who had been produced on off-Broadway, an intellectual, and he had achieved a certain individual flair of his own. He had also launched *Grand Street*, a literary quarterly.

Things were changing around the Gramercy Park area,

and the owner of 19 Gramercy Park South had more time to become conscious of them and moreover to do something about it. In the late 1960s, a 108-year-old building, the Friends Meeting House, facing the park just east of the Sonnenberg house, had come under threat of demolition. The handsome, simple, but austere building between Irving Place and Third Avenue on Twentieth Street had been used only sporadically by the Quaker organization that owned it. That group, the New York Meeting of the Religious Society of Friends, had transferred their principal activities to the headquarters at Stuyvesant Square, a half-dozen blocks away.

When the Quakers signed a contract to sell the building for five hundred thousand dollars to a builder who planned to convert it to an apartment house, Ben got busy. With three friends and neighbors, he formed the Meeting House Foundation to take action that would block the razing. The structure was already an official landmark, designated as such by the Landmarks Preservation Commission in 1965. Nonetheless, because it served no practical purpose by being empty, the building could legally be demolished.

Ben huddled with his colleagues. They were an impressive group. Mrs. Max Ascoli, the wife of the publisher of the *Reporter* magazine, was the daughter of Julius Rosenwald, the Chicago merchant who had been one of the owners of Sears, Roebuck and Company. Armand G. Erpf, an especially close friend of Ben's, was a senior partner of Carl M. Loeb, Rhoades & Company, one of Wall Street's top brokerage houses. And Jerome Straka, who was the president and chief executive officer of Chesebrough-Pond's.

They developed a strategy and pursued it two ways. They worked on the sentiments of the Quakers, trying to convince them that the building was too historic, too much part of the Gramercy Park scene, to be allowed to disappear. They worked on the builder, using the same emotional theme but also emphasizing that, under the provisions of a landmark designation, the reconstruction would be unusually complex and expensive. The two-pronged offensive succeeded. The Friends lowered the price of the property to four hundred thousand dollars, and the builder agreed to void his purchase contract with them. The Meeting House Foundation, headed by Sonnenberg, bought the venerable building.

When he was contacted by reporters afterward, Ben informed them that the plan was to turn the structure into a cultural center, but beyond that details were unclear as yet.

"All we wanted to do," Ben said, "was to get married to this place first. Then we will hire an architect to put some paint and a new dress on the old girl. There's no reason why she can't be quite a lively landmark."

The efforts proved successful and today the building serves as a cultural center.

There were other, similar projects in which he involved himself. The plain fact was that, although this new phase of his life "was all him, it wasn't as exciting nor did it have the pressures that would naturally have flowed from it," said Ted Kheel, the labor arbitrator who was a longtime Sonnenberg friend. Sonnenberg could still involve himself in anything that pleased or titillated him. He could still be the publicist extraordinaire, the social adviser, the patron of the arts, the host to writers, Broadway and movie stars, or the participant in community activities. "He was having fun, as much or more in his retirement as before," said Ted Kheel. "It pleased him to sit in glory in his house or take that front table at 21 and know that he had created an indelible identity. Personally, I think he was unique. He could play that game and no one could take it away from him when he would say, in so many words, 'This is a little, grimy boy from the Lower East Side and look at what I've done.' No one.

"His home was so ludicrous that it was spectacular. He had lots of very interesting things, but many were showier than they were valuable. He had a lot of junk in there, too. Brass, which was very showy, is not expensive. He did have some good paintings, but the apparent opulence of the house was overdone, too much without relief. But the pine-paneled room was magnificent. His furniture looked great, but lots of it was late reproduction English. Ben didn't kid himself about any of it, though. He enjoyed it for its effect, but inside it really didn't affect him so that he thought he was much better than anyone else. He knew that the effect of what he did or had was probably greater than its intrinsic value or meaning.

"In that sense," Kheel said, "he reminded me of another fabulous character, Michael Quill, the president of the Transit Workers Union in New York. Quill would often say or do something outrageous and the newspapers would put it on page one. 'Look at those idiots,' Quill would say. 'They put this shit on page one!' He was having fun and so was Ben. Ben could look at himself, laugh, and say, 'Isn't this incredible!' "

As he reached sixty-five and seventy approached quickly, Ben found the time to reminisce over past triumphs and planned some new ones. The descriptive label he put on each captured its essence:

Creative—If John Cameron Swazey could be an effective television personality and spokesman for Timex Watches, Bob Hope (Ben's great friend) could be a timeless spokesman for Pepsodent and then a myriad group of other products. And if Frank Borman, the astronaut and board chairman of Eastern Airlines, could be the TV personification of that troubled airline, why not Charles A. Lindbergh, probably America's most beloved aviator, as spokesman for Pan American Airways? Juan Trippe, Pan Am's chief, was agreeable and so was "Lindy." It was a successful tieup. Thinking big never hurt.

Opportunistic—Expanding his growing foothold on Wall Street, Ben secured an appointment with the redoubtable Harold Bache, the head of Bache and Company. Bache greeted him with his own public-relations man. Ben tried to be gracious but couldn't prevent himself from asking, "Have you ever considered the benefit of public relations?"

Bache gave him a frosty stare. "Of course, we have," he said. "Why do you think we employ this gentleman?" nodding toward his P.R. man, who was shaking with anger.

Sonnenberg stared at them with the lofty glare of a parent aroused at his siblings' naiveté. He sighed deeply. "Harold," he said, "when was the last time you were on the cover of *Time* magazine?"

"Why, I—I've never been on the cover of *Time*. Why would I?" sputtered Bache. "Why would they put a stockbroker on the cover? I've never heard of it."

"Harold, may I use your phone?" Sonnenberg asked. He dialed and then said, "Jeanette, call Harry Luce at *Time*. Tell him I want him to come to my office in forty minutes."

As he hung up, Harold Bache's eyes bulged. Henry Luce was the publisher of *Time*, and he was "Harry" only to his most intimate friends. He asked, as Ben plopped his homburg on his head and got into his Chesterfield, "Will he come, Son-nenberg? Can *you* do that?"

Ben paused at the door, a dapper, 150-percent-contained figure. "He will, Harold," he said, "and *I* can."

Luce begged off, *Time* never ran Bache on its cover, but Sonnenberg got a fifty-thousand-dollar fee to represent the stockbroker for a six-month period.

Truncating—Attending a business convention, Sonnenberg spied an excessively tall conventioneer whose evident self-satisfaction seemed to match his height. Ben inquired about him and learned that "Mr. Tall" was the president of a successful manufacturing business in the Midwest. The publicist studied the producer as he strode through the lobby and the convention rooms and couldn't resist the temptation. He approached the businessman, introduced himself, and told him, "Well, people are right. We are definitely look-alikes."

Mr. Tall gazed down with amazement on Ben's shiny pate, easily a foot below him. "Now, that's strange, friend," the manufacturer said. "I would have sworn there was something different about us."

Mr. Short grinned up at the friendly but puzzled face. "Well, maybe so. Maybe there are some indefinable differences between us," said Ben. "But I like to think that there are many similarities between successful people."

"That's reasonable," said Mr. Tall, getting friendlier.

Ben reached up, placing an arm on the other's shoulder. "Good," he said. "You know, it's strange about successful people. Some are successful because of things that they do and others because of things that they don't do. In my long career as an adviser to many businessmen, I have learned that they are two distinct species."

The midwesterner stopped short. He was evidently both intrigued and annoyed in equal proportions. "Well, I'd sure like to know which one of those—those species I am," he asserted.

Ben grinned. He had hooked him, and all he had to do now was to pull him in. "Are you—is your success similar to that of the Ukrainian farmer who achieved quite a reputation around the countryside as a crack marksman?" he asked. "When they finally got him to confess, the farmer admitted that what he did was to take aim at any old tree in the forest, close his eyes, and pull the trigger. Then he would go out into the forest and seek a bullet hole. When he found one on a tree, he drew bull's-eyes around it. That's how he obtained his reputation as a marksman."

Silence fell between them. After some moments, Mr. Tall, the manufacturer, smiled down at Mr. Short, the publicist, and said, "You know, that's downright fascinating. I'd like to hear more about it. I guess we are a lot the same, after all. Let me buy you a drink."

Influential—In 1972, when Jim Bowling announced to Ben that he was going to Australia, Sonnenberg's eyes took on the twinkle that had become so familiar to his friends. As Bowling said later, "It was, I like to think, one of Ben's most characteristic traits, a cheerful, upbeat, sort of marvelous twinkle. It was as if he had suddenly discovered something that had an unusual insight."

"If you are planning to go there," Ben said, "you have to meet the Lady Fairfax. She is a most attractive, gracious woman."

"The Lady Fairfax?"

"Yes, the wife of Sir Warwick Fairfax. He is a great gentleman and the owner of major newspapers, television stations, radio stations, magazines, and other properties, all in Australia."

"Quite a figure, isn't he? One of the press lords."

"The press lord there. I will write to her and tell her you are coming."

Would it help? Bowling wondered to himself. Could Ben actually smooth his way so far from home? But when he arrived down under, Bowling found himself whisked through customs VIP-style, and as he emerged he was approached by a man who announced, "The Lady Fairfax would like you to come to her home for dinner this evening. She is entertaining the prime minister."

When Jim returned to New York, his account of that dinner brought back Ben's twinkle in "all its elfin glory."

There were other cases where Ben had used his influence in the public domain. Asked by Brooke Astor, the president of the Astor Foundation which was a contributor to the New York Public Library, to aid in building a new top infrastructure for the library, Ben first got Richard Salomon, who had sold his business, Charles of the Ritz. Salomon then pressed into service on an honorary basis Andrew Heiskell, the publisher of *Time* Magazine, who in turn got Vartan Gregorian to accept the post of paid president. Sonnenberg was also helpful in placing Charles Ryskamp as director of the Pierpont Morgan Library. And it was Brooke Astor, whose foundation was also a contributor to the Morgan Library, who had told him with a gleaming smile, "Just think, Ben. You will always live on in both those institutions for what you did for them."

Obfuscatory—There was really no doubt about it. For many years he had enjoyed startling certain people, especially those with a stuffy nature or with an astronomical opinion of their own diction, with involved, elephantine statements that could only leave them reeling. It had started with his early predilection for the long, twisting sentences Dickens and Thackeray used to tell a story. The English, of course, had changed, preferring the more clipped rhetoric of an Evelyn Waugh, C. P. Snow, and Graham Greene. But, even in his later years, Sonnenberg liked the hyperbole, the flowing phrase, and the long sentence. In addition, he liked to throw in a bit of a hook. And it would all be delivered in a deadpan manner.

At a dinner party in Manhattan, Ben found himself sitting across the table from Sir Harold Nicolson, the famous British diplomat, historian, and biographer. Nearby sat Alistair Cooke, a friend of both. Ben kept staring at Sir Harold, apparently trying to figure out if the former member of the House of Commons was as totally buttoned up as he appeared. Not at all nonplused by the continuing stare, Sir Harold looked back calmly. Finally, he stirred and asked Ben a question about New York City. Taking a deep breath, Sonnenberg launched into a colorful, serpentine reply that resembled a many-colored, verbal mosaic. As Ben spoke, the Englishman's face turned redder and redder. When Ben finished, he waited for Sir Harold's reply. It came slowly, haltingly.

"I'm sorry, Mr. —," he said, "I seem to have lost something in translation. I'm terribly sorry, I —"

As Alistair Cooke put it, "My countryman must have thought Ben was one of the strangest, rudest, stupidest men he had ever met. Actually, Sonnenberg was running rings around Nicolson's mind and simply using an idiom of humor that Nicolson had never heard before."

As for Ben, he had had a fine time that evening, including, of course, the repartee at the table.

Sometimes Sonnenberg wondered if he could be a success again with a big agency in his style of some thirty-five years. Not that he wanted to. After all, he was over seventy at that point; but it was natural to wonder, when a man looks back in the twilight of his life and sees everything changing but not really. A stubborn core of him, basic pride without doubt, assured him that he could do it all over again. Another side— the real man reinforced by the keen hindsight of years and years of sweet-sour experience—convinced him that he would not have done it with an agency at all if he had known then the joys of independent operations. He had never really enjoyed the nitty-gritty of the business. But he had always enjoyed the challenge of getting under the surface of people and situations and engineering ways of maximizing the former's faculties and the latter's potential. Nowadays, he knew that it was all laid out first on paper; dreams given names, numbers, deadlines, and even occasionally cost-effective ratios. As if you could capture a dream and enclose it in an eight-by-eleven-inch cage.

Even in the earlier years, it was necessary to go through that formality. Today, every presentation is submitted to a committee, but in those days he enjoyed a personal kind of relationship with clients. Occasionally, however, he would come into the working part of the agency and tell the staff, "We have this new, panting client. Give him something in writing to keep him at bay for a while." He would throw out a few ideas, usually perfunctory at that stage, and the wordsmiths would put it together. Then it would go over to the client, who might or might not—usually not—read it. The real campaign would develop from a series of meetings, as often as not, some conversations over lunch or dinner or parties at the house. And then his staff would really get to work implementing it.

No, he mused, there had been nothing in his time like today's multilevel agency system and structured meetings. He had no time clocks and no Monday morning meetings or "plans board" meetings, as the larger agencies of today have. Their style is to call in the newspaper division, the radio di-

vision, the television division. In his day, he reminded himself, everyone was a media *maven*, a total media specialist.
You did everything and learned a lot more. And enjoyed it
more.

Thinking about it, he sighed and sipped his glass of hot
tea, wondering why people thought bigness and busyness
meant better. What was important was to get into the viscera
of the situation and see whether something different could be
done, something with panache or pizazz. The public-relations
efforts these days were so cut-and-dried, as though the prac-
titioners were more afraid of being labeled "press agents" than
concerned with making their clients appear distinctive. Was
it that they really didn't know "how to polish the escutcheon"? Or was it simply that they were dedicated to upgrading
the profession?

What had happened to the art of being artful?

It was all part of the game in those post–World War II
years—the formative forties, fifties, and sixties—when the
good, old U.S.A. showed its heels to everyone. You worked the
street, worked the beat, learning the turf and all its characters. You looked at the world as it was and as it might be all
in terms of your client, and you applied creative energy, using
your God-given instincts. Conversely, today's "exposure prac-
titioners," the men in the big corporate agencies, were really
a crew of dull fellows. They had little flair, the classic B-school
sort of guys, who appeared to get a kind of visceral pleasure
from emulating the button-down CEOs who were their clients.
He knew, of course, that some people referred to him as "a
pirate." Well, so be it. If "pirate" meant being colorful, creative, aggressive, manipulative, then fine, he was certainly a
pirate. The unadulterated truth was that somehow in every
situation he knew how to put things together, he had a sense
of who to rub together with whom, a sense of knowing how
they would interact and of what might come from that. Had
the need for all that changed? Of course not; it never would.

Or had it? He well knew that some of the younger agency
entrepreneurs regarded him as old hat, a relic whose time was
long past, but he knew that some of the others idolized him,
putting him on a sort of pedestal as a communicator nonpar-
eil. Those with a negative opinion of him were only defending
themselves and their way of functioning. Oh, he knew what

they said: that the chief executives he knew and hobnobbed with were aging, just as he was aging. He was no longer needed. As more marketing executives, more lawyers, more financial men assumed the chief executive's mantle, as different disciplines move to the top, the old ignorance about communications was replaced by more professional experience. It wasn't just public relations anymore, but advertising, sales promotion, product marketing. Who then needed an accommodator; or a troubleshooter when there was trouble? No one, the critics insisted.

Then there were the other sages, the ones who claimed that the Sonnenbergs, the Edward Bernays, or the Ivy Lees and the T. J. Rosses were not unique, but merely products of their time. Each generation, these sages claimed, necessarily produced different kinds of people to suit its different needs. But that sort of attitude, he knew, was especially dangerous. If you assumed that as fact, you also assumed that people changed, which was never the case. They remained as ornery and as gentle, as confused and also as wise, as petty and yet as magnanimous as they had always been.

Ben began to doze in his chair. He knew it through almost closed eyes. Leonard Horn, his butler, peeked in, saw him sitting there with his glass of tea perilously suspended in his hand, gently removed the glass, and tiptoed out.

Much as he liked the wit and poise of the English poets, philosophers and novelists, he wasn't so sure that he always agreed with their homilies and their frequent, dour outlook, a point of view that probably had a lot to do with bad weather and faulty digestion. In the 1970s, Hilda and Helen urged him to take better care of himself—he was after all nearing seventy-five. So he stayed home more, put up his feet, pondered more, read more. The leisure gave him the opportunity to express to himself or to visitors—not that he really needed the opportunity—to indulge his own acid wit, a way of looking at people, places and things with a cold, sometimes icy eye.

About Frank Saunders, the former Sonnenberg colleague who had had more than his share of family illness, Ben said, "He is the guy who always steps on the banana peel."

To Jay Scott, a Sonnenberg staffer, who one day came into the office wearing argyle socks, he remarked, "I hope you choose your words better than your socks."

On his old friend Albert Lasker, the Chicago advertising man: "Before I met Albert Lasker, I was always seen with beautiful blondes. After I met with Albert Lasker, I was always seen with Albert Lasker."

About the Berlins, the people not the city: "I know the difference between Isaiah Berlin and Irving Berlin, and I know them both."

When he was often urged to write his memoirs, he would answer, "I don't know how to write. There's a difference between a gag and an essay."

On press agentry: "I am the last of the old school. It's now done by machine. There's not a literate man in the business."

On the public-relations business: "Public relations is the practice of popular persuasion. Its method is to make the planned seem spontaneous, accidental, natural, instead of posed. The most important ingredient in public relations is timing. What is heroic in one hour may be villainous in the next, and yet an hour later may again prove heroic."

And so he sort of sauntered through the twilight of his life, slower physically than he had been but as mentally sharp as ever. He would call in hot tips to his favorite journalists, such as Bob Bedingfield at the *New York Times* (who mostly didn't use them); or make a merger, such as between Neiman-Marcus and Carter Hawley Hale Stores of Los Angeles (it happened, but Sonnenberg was only one of several matchmakers); or plot corporate and investment strategy with his growing coterie of Wall Street clients and friends (with whom much of it worked).

He would, with very little advance notice, announce that he was either going to England for two weeks or not going to England for two weeks. Not that he enjoyed canceling appointments or trips—he had never been a chronic canceler like some, who built up and talked up a trip and the night before discovered publicly that they were too, too busy to make it. It was fun, too, as he told a number of people, to shrug off many of his old habits. It gave him a nice, light feeling of freedom.

Of Ben in those last few years, Jim Bowling, who had

lunch with Sonnenberg at least once a month through the late 1970s, said, "What I would normally do was to go down there, usually for lunch. There would be some sort of focus that either I would need or Ben would have in mind. Most times, it would involve some problems or it would be just to outline a situation or something that was coming up. I wanted to get his counsel on what he thought we ought to do or how he would analyze what might happen in circumstances that were important to us at Philip Morris. Invariably, he gave you a good perspective, a philosophical one and a historical one. . . . It was an incredible treat to go there. I loved visiting with Ben. It was just like a mental bath. You came away stimulated and refreshed. The elegance of the whole thing was kind of marvelous. He had a great mind, even in those days. He was fun. . . ."

14

THE CURTAIN FALLS

Sonnenberg didn't believe in death. It didn't travel in the same circles he did. It was simply not part of his world. Death was for other people who had no other recourse than to give in to it. It was not for his good friends, his best clients, his media pals. Certainly it was not for his family and most surely not for him. He savored the old folk tale in which the angel of death could not tag a wily old Jew because every time the angel caught up with him the man assumed a different disguise and different accent.

Naturally, he had experienced trauma over the deaths of friends and colleagues: George Schreiber, Jack Pacey, Bobby Lehman, John O'Hara, Willy Maugham. Although their passings affected him deeply when they occurred, he would abruptly cease his mourning. He would not, if the impossible ever became possible, want anyone to mourn him for too long.

It was life that should be celebrated, not death. All those great friends who had gone on would remain immortal to him, a source of permanent joy. Their deaths, much as they were to be regretted, were just curtains that had been drawn over their lives, which would always vibrate with vitality.

As a result, when in 1974 and 1975 people began to observe that Sonnenberg's face was somewhat sallower than before, that he had grown thinner and had developed a persistent hoarseness, Ben had to endure their solicitude. He blithely told his joke about the man who fooled the angel of death. He was scarcely concerned. His health, despite his pale complexion, pudgy figure, pipe-smoking and complete lack of exercise, had always been superb. He could not bring himself to see the changes others noticed as symptomatic of anything serious. And he said so.

When those changes turned into symptoms of something worrisome, he still kept it from his friends. Later, Jim Bowling observed, "I never really thought of him as being sick." Ted Kheel would call and be told that Ben was "indisposed." The labor lawyer, accustomed to years of hemming and hawing and prevarications of all sorts, began to suspect what was going on, and he was worried. Alistair Cooke had some trepidations, but his weekly dinners with Ben continued for the most part. Ben said little about his health, and Cooke was too much the English gentleman to raise the embarrassing subject.

Ben, in the meantime, was having a round of examinations. He was hoarse, he had pain, and he was losing weight. Finally, the diagnosis came in. It was dire. He had throat cancer. But it wasn't necessarily fatal. With chemotherapy, he could live on for a long time. But Sonnenberg knew better. The impossible had become not only possible, but certain. Hilda, Helen, and Ben, Jr., were very distressed. He tried to bolster their feelings. Perhaps he would make it, after all, but if he didn't, they were not to fret. He had had a long, wonderful, totally gratifying life. And he could still function, keeping that curtain suspended.

He still went out, on a limited scale, and met people. He lunched and dined in his usual places or invited some friends to his house. But there were times as 1976 passed into 1977 when the pain was growing greatly. He went into the hospital for a short stay, then again, insisting on a male rather than female nurse. The hospital routine and bureaucracy annoyed him. A fastidious man, he didn't like staying in a building where privacy gave way to medical need, and he didn't like being in the same surroundings with other sick people. During one stay there, he got up, dressed himself over the protests of his male nurse, and walked out, taking a cab home.

Undaunted by it all, he continued some of his business and cultural activities. But he was becoming more frail, the chemotherapy sapping him of his strength for days at a time. The new year, 1977, came and went, his situation obviously worsening in spite of the treatment. In January 1978, he decided to give a party to provide a proper sendoff for a "Royal Heritage" series to be presented by Huw Weldon, a producer at the Public Broadcasting Network. After the party at his house, Ben would accompany the group to the Morgan Library nearby, where others would join his guests for a more formal presentation.

"I came into Ben's house," recalled Alistair Cooke, "and saw Ben. He looked quite ill. He had always had a sallow complexion, he was never really pink, and whenever you said, 'How are you?' he would reply, 'Fine, fine.' Or if he had a little cold, he would say, 'Got a little cold.' He had extraordinary health, most of his life. But the first time I ever heard him say that he hadn't was that evening when I came to the top of the second-floor stairs and I said to him, amid the babble of people and the clinking of glasses, 'How are you, Ben?' he said, 'Lousy.' He didn't go with the rest of us to the Morgan Library that night. He wasn't up to it."

The unhappy word was getting around. About the same time, Alden Whitman, probably the finest obituary writer the *New York Times* had had in decades, began preparing an advance obituary on Sonnenberg. It was a longtime practice of the *Times* to do so when celebrities had a serious illness. Whitman visited some people who knew Sonnenberg well, including Frank Saunders, who had worked for the Sonnenberg Agency before moving to Ruder & Finn and later to Philip Morris as its public relations director. Saunders, who had only occasionally seen Sonnenberg or members of the family in recent years, did not know how seriously ill Ben was. "Are you doing an article on Sonnenberg?" Saunders asked Whitman, whom he had never met before.

"I'll tell you the truth," Whitman said with a hesitant smile. "I'm writing an obituary on Ben to prepare for his possible death."

Saunders was shocked. "My God," he said, "I didn't realize that the *Times* did that."

"Oh, yes," Whitman told him. "That's my beat. I prepare these things and they sit there ready on the bank in the composing room."

Sonnenberg's distress at his own condition was complicated by some bad news involving his son. Ben, Jr., had contracted a serious, debilitating disease, which relegated him to a wheelchair and, in addition, his son's marriage was foundering. Ben and Hilda, already suffering considerable anguish over Ben's condition, were distraught. Life, after smiling at them for decades, had turned sour.

But Ben rallied. After finishing a series of chemotherapy treatments, he began to feel a bit better. And with it came a geometric expansion of his personal zest. When, at the end of May 1978 Alistair Cooke phoned to ask if he would like to have dinner with him and a friend of his, a music producer for the British Broadcasting Company who was helping Cooke to prepare a history of jazz and American popular songs, Sonnenberg readily agreed. The producer had already met Ben. They went down to the Sonnenberg house for drinks with Ben, and Alistair Cooke took them both out to dinner. The visitor was an antiques collector, and he and Ben had a very pleasant evening discussing antiques and British and American mores. Cooke thought that he had rarely seen Sonnenberg in better form, except for his very pale complexion and a curious resonance in his voice. He was just being himself and the producer was delighted. Afterward, the man told Cooke, "I've never met a human being quite like that."

A few weeks later, Ben picked himself up, though he felt poorly again, and visited the great antiques auctions in London. When in August Brendan Gill came to see him, he was stunned to learn that Ben, in his dire state, had gone there. "To a collector," Ben explained with his elfin smile, "buying is living."

On July 4, 1978, Jane and Alistair Cooke had a farewell dinner with Ben before they took off for a month in England. They never saw him again. When they returned to New York, they went to Gramercy Park several times in the hope of seeing him. But he was too frail to have visitors. Each time, they just sat and talked with Hilda and Helen.

The last time they were there, Helen said she would go up to tell Ben that the Cookes were there and wanted to see him. She returned and said that her father had told her that he very much wanted to see Jane and Alistair, but he just wasn't up to it.

A few days later, however, Ben phoned Alistair. In a shockingly frail voice, "like paper," said Cooke, "he told me that the doctor said it was just a question of more appetite and more weight." But he had no appetite and he was losing weight.

On September 5, 1978, Ben Sonnenberg was admitted to Lenox Hill Hospital in Manhattan. The next day, at 8:14 in the morning, he died.

"I direct that my body be cremated without any ceremony or memorial service whatsoever.

"I direct my executors as soon as practicable after my death to destroy all data, files and correspondence which they may not require in connection with the administration of my estate . . ."

So, in that will dated December 7, 1977, and admitted to probate October 3, 1978, he drew the final curtain on his life. Because he had directed his executors to liquidate all his files, the family decided that it would not cooperate with any biographer, although Helen told this writer that she might "someday" change her mind.

The body was cremated on September 7, the day after death, at the Garden State Cemetery, in North Bergen, New Jersey. But it was odd that destiny cooperated with Sonnenberg's order that a veil cover his seventy-seven years of life and more than half-century as a professional image maker. He died about a month after New York City's three newspapers became embroiled in an eighty-eight-day strike, which halted their publication until early December. The long-prepared obituary never appeared in the *Times* or any New York newspaper, although the *Times*'s news service forwarded the obituary, written by John Hess, who had succeeded Alden Whitman, to many of its member newspapers, some of which carried a smaller obituary around the country. When the *Times* resumed publication, it carried two full pages of obituaries of those prominent people who had died during the strike. Sonnenberg received only four paragraphs.

Because of all this, many people who had worked for him, knew him, or socialized with him, or, for that matter many of his clients, never knew that he had died until later.

Why did Sonnenberg want his life to remain a closed book after his death? The paradox of an internationally known publicist, who dressed, lived, and entertained in a manner designed to attract attention, not wanting to open his papers to an observer or biographer seem too odd to let pass without examination. By consensus, his closest friends and associates are convinced that he simply decided that "his show was over, let's strike the set." He had always claimed, they say, that he didn't want any personal publicity, that the famous 1950 *New Yorker* piece was quite enough. Besides, although he sometimes violated his own advice on not gossiping about clients, friends, or acquaintances, he felt that permitting his papers to be studied might violate confidences that he wanted to keep with clients. One or two believe that he himself had dealings that he preferred to take to the grave with him.

There is some feeling, too, that his conviction that he wanted all talk about his life to end with his death was indicated by his order in his will that most of his collection be auctioned, rather than retained either by his family or some institution or museum. Was it just a matter of ego? That was probably an important element in his decision. He had built his accumulation of art, brass, sculpture, china, and furniture painstakingly over the years not only for the pleasure it gave him, but as a means of impressing others. Why should he want to pass it on to someone else who might use it in the same way, or worse, misuse it?

It's likely, too, that Sonnenberg—who callously at times said of friends who were going downhill, "It's a shame, it's too bad, let's forget it because there's nothing we can do about it"—was so distressed over his own deteriorating situation that he really didn't care to have anyone examine his life or keep his collection intact.

Perhaps, also, he chose his course because he was so unhappy to leave it all—his colorful life, his fascinating experiences, the fabulous art—that he abhorred the idea of anyone else "having it."

After having spent more than two years researching Sonnenberg, I have my own version of why he elected to do what he did. He was just being consistent, being the individualist, the picturesque personality, the guy with the odd twinkle, when he ordered his body cremated, no memorial service be held, and all his papers be destroyed. It was characteristic of him to do things that set him apart from others: the way he dressed, the elaborate way he often spoke, his magnificently gaudy house, the unique way he lorded his affluence over his clients by living better than they did—and inviting them over to see it. Perhaps he sensed how difficult, if not impossible, it would be for anyone to capture him just as he was, or to enjoy his assets in the manner he did or in the way they deserved.

In his will, filed in the Surrogate's Court in the County of New York, there were a few surprises.

He left Hilda 15 percent of his "tangible property" and directed his executors that the balance be sold at auction and the proceeds added to his residuary estate. The residuary estate was to be divided into "Share A" and "Share B." Share A was bequeathed to the trustees, George Weissman and Helen, who were also the executors, to invest for the use of Hilda during her lifetime. Share B was to be divided into two equal parts, "Part One" and "Part Two." One-half of Part One was to go to Helen and the other half was to be put in trust for her. Part Two was to go to Ben, Jr., but was to be put in trust by the trustees, invested, and the proceeds to be paid to him.

The entire estate, incidentally, was given only the token estimate in the will of "valued at more than $500,000." But, in actuality, the estate had a value, as proven later, of more than $5 million.

In the will, Ben "forgave the indebtedness" of his two children and left to each an amount equal to each one's indebtedness to him. He left twenty thousand dollars to each of his five grandchildren. And he left twenty thousand dollars to

Jeanette Blader, his longtime secretary who later became secretary to George Weissman at Philip Morris; twenty thousand dollars to Leonard D. Horn, the Sonnenberg butler; and ten thousand dollars to Inez Jenkins, Hilda's personal maid of many years' service.

As "a memento of me," he left twenty-five hundred dollars to three godsons: John Justin Rex Metcalf, the son of John Metcalf, an English friend of Ben's; Adam Paley, son of Stuart Paley, a friend of Ben's, the son of William Paley of Columbia Broadcasting Company, and a New York lawyer; and Alexander Powers, the son of Ralph Powers, a friend and neighbor who lived at 24 Gramercy Park South.

Ben bequeathed directly to the Metropolitan Museum of Art the "Holy Family," a 9½-inch-by-12½-inch pen-and-sepia drawing by da Cortona. It was one of his most beloved pieces of art and the only one he left directly to a museum.

Considerable excitement grew over the scheduled auction of the Sonnenberg art and antique collection, due to be carried on for four consecutive days, from June 6 to 9, at Sotheby Parke Bernet's Manhattan gallery. Six months earlier, in December 1978, Parke Bernet had trumpeted the event: "It is expected to be one of the most glamourous Manhattan auctions in modern times." A few days before Christmas that year, Paul Goldberger, the architecture critic of the *New York Times*, whom Sonnenberg had told others years before was "a young man to watch," visited the mansion and found Leonard Horn outside the house, polishing the lion-headed, front-door knocker as though nothing had changed. Sonnenberg had been gone more than three months and Goldberger's curiosity drew this answer from the butler: "It is what he would have wanted. We want to keep the house going the way it always was." The architecture critic then proceeded to take his readers through a meticulous tour of the house, pausing to point out various pieces and to sum up the virtues and faults of each room.

A month later, Rita Reif, the *Times*'s antiques writer, wrote in her column, "The most impressive auction of English antiques to be held in New York in many years is many months away, but collectors are already talking. . . . The importance of this sale increased substantially in December after an even more remarkable collection assembled by Gerald

Hochschild, the Chilean mining millionaire, was sold at Sotheby's in London. That sale established a new high for English furniture when a weighty wonder of a Chippendale desk sold for $196,000; it is now owned by Ronald Lauder, vice president of Estee Lauder, the cosmetics concern."

Also in January 1979, Arthur Spiegelman of Reuters News Service wrote, "The auction sale is expected to be one of the biggest in the city's history. The valuables collected by the late Benjamin Sonnenberg are expected to be sold for up to $4 million, according to Sotheby Parke Bernet. Sotheby's say it will be the sale of the year. . . .''

Prior to the auction, the Sonnenberg house was placed on sale at an asking price of $1.9 million. The notice, for those whose appetite had already been well whetted, served as yet another dramatic event in the sale of the Sonnenberg estate.

A month before the Sotheby auction, media anticipation hardly lagged. *Town & Village*, a New York weekly, observed, "The sale of the Sonnenberg collections is scheduled as a grand finale to the New York auction season, which ends during June."

Twice, again preauction, Rita Reif came to the fore. On June 1, she declared that "the Benjamin Sonnenberg collection of art and antiques—one of the largest (1,762 lots) and most valuable (it may total $3 to $4 million) ever sold at auction in America—goes on view today and under the hammer Tuesday through Saturday at Sotheby Parke Bernet, Madison Avenue at 76th Street. The presale exhibition, which will open today through Monday, 10 A.M. to 5 P.M., is the most sizable ever held in the auction concern's commodious headquarters. Envision the contents of a five-story, 37-room, generously appointed town house jammed into Sotheby's eight galleries."

And on the opening day, Tuesday, June 6, she wrote:

The four-day presale exhibition of the collection attracted near-record crowds of 4,000 on Friday and Saturday. About 600 additional persons paid $35 to see the collection Friday night at the party held to benefit the Decorative Arts Trust and the New York Public Library. By late yesterday, a total of nearly 12,000 had filed through Sotheby's to examine the contents. . . . What they saw were eight galleries filled to capacity.

. . . It was the largest exhibition staged at Sotheby's, and the catalogue of the sale reflected this fact. The two-volume document is the heaviest, thickest and costliest for a single sale produced by the house. But sales at $12 for each volume have been so brisk, it may soon be a collector's item, even though 11,000 copies, a record number, were printed. . . . The dispersal of this huge assemblage of furnishings, which took five weeks to pack and move, will cover nine sessions. There are already more than 1,000 advance bids on lots up for sale from those who cannot attend or do not wish to bid openly. . . .

The auction in that summer of 1979 was an outstanding success both financially and in terms of the excitement it created. The largest collection of art and antiques from a single owner ever auctioned by Sotheby's brought almost $5 million. The sum was the third highest for any single collection to be sold by Sotheby's, followed only by the Norton Simon sales in 1971 and 1973, which brought $12.7 million and the Geraldine Rockefeller Dodge collection, which drew $7.5 million in 1975 and 1976.

But the eclat it created, attracting more bids, buyers, and spectators than the auction house had ever had, was tremendous. About thirty thousand people attended, including many who had never turned out at an auction before. More than eight thousand bids were received from buyers who couldn't attend even before the sale commenced, many not only from the United States but from thirteen other countries as well. Even before the nine-day series ended, John L. Marion, Sotheby's U.S. chairman, said that 25 percent of the lots had been bought by people who had never before bought at Sotheby's. Of the 1,762 lots put on the block, only eighteen did not sell, and some successful bids set world records.

As Marion jubilantly told Rita Reif, "This is Ben's biggest party, which he's thrown open to the public, and they've come and enjoyed the feast." Staring at the standing-room-only crowd that had jammed into the final afternoon session, he told her, "He would have been delighted at the number of new people that he's infected with the same collecting bug that he had."

Many well-known people attended: Mike Nichols, the movie and stage director; Brooke Hayward, the actress and writer; Robert Vaughan, the actor; Paul Simon, the singer; Senator Daniel P. Moynihan, New York's Democratic senator; Clay Felker, the magazine publisher; Lee Radziwill, the socialite sister of Jacqueline Onassis. And, of course, there were Ben's best friends, including Brendan Gill and Alistair Cooke. As Rita Reif reported, there was even one Leonard Sonnenberg, a Long Island chemicals producer who had never met Ben, but who came because he shared the same name. He left with five brass pieces for which he had paid $225.

As expected, the stellar pieces drew the highest bids. The Coe Kerr Gallery of New York paid the highest price for any piece when it shelled out $210,000 for the John Singer Sargent painting of the Dutchess of Sutherland. It was also the highest price ever paid for any Sargent work. A Paris dealer paid $82,000 for a Seurat crayon drawing believed to be of the artist's mother and sister. Albert Giacometti's bust of Diego, his brother, sold for $77,000 to David Wingate, a New York producer of steel parts. A fine Queen Anne inlaid burr walnut estate table, circa 1710, drew $26,000. A George I–style burr walnut cabinet sold for $7,000. An Urbino Istoriato dish, dated 1546, brought $23,000. And a pair of fine jars, Faenza Maiolica Albarelli, circa 1500–1520, sold for $32,000.

A month after the auction, the Sonnenberg mansion was purchased for $1.5 million by the Baron Langer Von Langerdoff, the German chemist who had created the New York perfume house of Evyan. Three years later, a perusal of the closed, empty house by this writer found it forlorn, full of debris, and strung with cobwebs—much, perhaps, as Hilda Sonnenberg saw it in 1931 when she hugged its wall to escape the rain.

On December 19, 1979, Hilda Sonnenberg died of cancer, also at the Lenox Hill Hospital, at seventy-seven, the same age as her husband when he had passed on. Three weeks after Ben's death, Hilda's daughter, Helen, had helped her move from the mansion into an apartment on East Seventy-ninth Street. Hilda had survived Ben by only fifteen months. The change in locale and the absence of her husband after fifty-two years may have had an adverse effect, as is common with older people taken out of their long-familiar environment or marital relationship or both. By common agreement, her husband's closest friends believe that Hilda never received the credit due her, mainly because her modest personality was so eclipsed by Ben's flamboyance. Her love, loyalty, her taste in home decor, which provided the background for Ben's avid collecting, her calm, quiet demeanor, and her ability to run a household around and yet encompass his business and social activities—all were viewed as of immense help and support to him. If he was "born old," so was she, and she indulged him and gave him the greatest license. If his partying excess sometimes wearied her and drove her to her bedroom, the theater, or a local movie, she was entitled to do so. But she had also served as a willing, gracious hostess over many years. And if at times she reacted to some of it with a covert smile, she was probably entitled to that, too.

15

A
FORWARD
LOOK
BACKWARD

Time, it seems, is lending a helping hand to Sonnenberg's wish to keep a veil over his long life. In the years since his death, many young men and women in the public-relations business have never heard of him or only vaguely recall hearing his name "somewhere." Most of his principal clients have passed on. Some who survived were reluctant to talk about him and became even more so as the years passed. His work for them had been too intimate, either on a professional or personal basis or both, or too unconventional for them to want to describe their relationship. Many of the middle-aged and senior public-relations people, of course, still remember him, but they, too, are getting older, retiring, or dying off. And, astonishingly, little had appeared about him in the media, at least during his lifetime, except for the 1950 *New Yorker* piece and some sundry pieces, so the written record is small and diminishing.

Will the Sonnenberg legend die?

One can be cynical and say "probably" or be naive and say "of course not." Most probably, as a publicist his name will be paired with those of his most famous clients—Charles Luckman of Lever Brothers, Sam Goldwyn of movie fame, John Snider of U.S. Industries, Henry and Margaret Rudkin of Pepperidge Farm, Fred Lazarus, Jr., of Federated Department Stores, Jerome Straka of Chesebrough-Pond's, Joseph Cullman and George Weissman of Philip Morris, Arthur Genet of Greyhound, and Robert Lehman of Lehman Brothers— either in passing references to their careers or in footnotes. Many of the significant things he did for them were known only between the two of them, or possibly a third party. That aside, his creative flair, *chutzpah*, and sheer zest in the art of personal and corporate image building will probably persist as a benchmark—or warning—of how it can be done or should not be done.

By comparison with today's more restrained, more inhibited, and no doubt more responsible practices in the field, his methods would be considered too feisty, too controversial, too calculated. But, it's just as likely that if he still lived and functioned as a professional, he would have adjusted to the changing times, the increased government scrutiny of corporations and corporate chiefs, to the more aware stockholders and the consumer advocates. And he probably would be as effective these days as he was in those.

If nothing else, Sonnenberg was as skilled a learner, with amazing retentiveness, as he was an accommodator and manipulator. In fact, some who observed him over many years wonder if Ben Sonnenberg was nothing more than a chameleonlike man who absorbed and adopted traits, customs, habits, and bits of culture and life style from different ages and especially from different people. It all started very early, when he decided as a youth that he wanted to be an Edwardian English gentleman and would dress and live that way, adding newly acquired detail as he became more sophisticated. He studied new acquaintances for something that he could use: the way they lifted a cup, crossed a knee, spoke, laughed, thought, or the impression they made when they entered a room. It was a lifelong process.

So, if the legend of Sonnenberg as a publicist is tenuous, it is reasonable that he would have at least held his own as a contemporary professional. The greater likelihood, however, is that, given his talents and ability to play "the levers of power," he would have risen to the top.

What about his other lives, the social host, the collector of arts and antiques, the invaluable consultant to the business elite, and the bon vivant? Of all of them, it's most likely that the legends that will be most durable are those involving his collecting, his skill as a host extraordinaire, and his appearance in the great restaurants, hotels, and resorts in this country and abroad. The dispersion of the art and antiques signifies that, although they no longer belong to Sonnenberg, his name will be part of their history and background. In art, that's known as provenance, meaning origin or source. As Brendan Gill observed in a retrospective article on the op-ed page of the *New York Times* almost a year after Sonnenberg's passing, referring to the art that adorned the walls of 19 Gramercy Park South, "In a sense, from now on he will belong to them and not they to him." The Sonnenberg Collection, in other words, will become an important name in provenances. But, in addition, his collection as an entity will probably also be long remembered for its size, scope, heterogeneity, eclecticism, especially when related to his unusual house.

His reputation as a social host will linger for a long time, not only because of his long expertise in that world, but because of the volume and brilliance of the many he had invited there over years. As other famous town houses fell under the wrecking ball and were converted to apartments, hotels, and office buildings, his remained and thrived. It was one of the most popular and busiest homes for social gatherings, some will insist the busiest in New York in those decades of the mid-twentieth century. Its plush service, the servants with white gloves, the glittering brass, the fine, if mixed, china— all imparted a memorable experience that should keep his reputation as a host glowing in a time of increasingly modest, more casual living.

As to his reputation as a bon vivant, that, too, lingers in

the minds and imaginations of those who service the fine restaurants, clubs, and hotels. The appearance of the slight, pudgy man in the old world clothes, with his boutonniere and the twinkle in his eye, reassured the maitre d', the waiters and waitresses, and the owners that there was still someone who appreciated gracious—and expensive—service. But these people are going, too, and that piquant memory no doubt will fade in time, although wisps of it may endure.

There's one aspect of Sonnenberg that, if nothing else, may be the basis for a lasting legend. It's simple and obvious—the "Sonnenberg collection," not the physical or cultural assets of his art collection, but the collection of his personal traits and pursuits that constituted Ben Sonnenberg himself. He will live on as a confidant of the mighty, the talented, the aspiring, and even the humble, as the personification of an earlier, more gilded age, as the molder of reputations of people and institutions, as the great collector, the epigram maker, author of the great one-liner, and as the attention-getting character on the scene. He was a throwback to an earlier time when an exuberant man of wealth could devote himself with style to art and hedonism. Few men of his time had as complex a personality and life. And he made it all palatable by making it obvious that he was partly a con man, partly a man filled with restless energy, and partly a man who had learned to twist destiny to his own ends. Even those who didn't like him, and there were more than a few, were compelled to admit that he was unforgettable, although not always pleasantly so.

The drawback was that he had too many different characteristics crowded into one person for everyone to accept and react to in the same way. It's easy to react to someone with one, two, or three dimensions—but twice that many? The reaction becomes entirely subjective. And fragmented. And varied.

For a final appraisal of Sonnenberg, two people were approached who had had long exposure to him, both close up and from a distance. One is Denny Griswold, founder and editor of *Public Relations News*, which she founded with her late husband, Glenn, in 1944. A business writer at *Business Week*, she met and married the boss, Griswold, worked briefly at the Sonnenberg Agency, and then launched her weekly. Mrs. Griswold, now married to J. Langdon Sullivan, probably knows more public-relations people in the United States and abroad than anyone else.

"I first met Ben in the late 1930s," Mrs. Griswold said, "when I was thinking of marrying Glenn. Since he was very much older than I was my family was raising hell about it. Ben then was courting both Glenn, who was editor-publisher of *Business Week*, and me. Somehow he found out about my personal problem. He knew a lot about people that he shouldn't have, but he did. He told me, 'Denny, we need you, come to work for me. If you're serious about forgetting this guy, it will help you if you left *Business Week* and came with me.' He was persuasive, one of the most persuasive men I ever met, and I made the move. But I married Glenn anyway.

"Ben was a good sport about it and even threw a party for us. But he couldn't resist a bit of a jab. When he came into the room, we immediately noticed a beautiful, dark, foreign-looking woman sitting there. Ben motioned toward her and told Glenn, so that I could hear it, 'She happens to be the current mistress of the king of Rumania. She's very sensual. If you're at all interested, Glenn, I can fix you up.' "

About a year later, Denny left the Sonnenberg Agency and shortly afterward started the weekly, which she has continuously published ever since. Over the years, she would meet Sonnenberg, hear about his exploits, and occasionally publish tidbits about him and his clients.

"His great forte, in my opinion, was that he understood people magnificently well," she said. "He could discern their weaknesses and their hidden longings and work on them. Did they want a fancy home, girls, media glamor, to meet celebrities or join the jet set? Everyone has a hidden dream, and everyone has a hidden hangup. He could supply the dream, and he knew how to soothe the hangup. His goal was to be well paid, and he was."

Sonnenberg was lavish in giving gifts to those who could be helpful to him, she added. But it tended to be short term unless the relationship remained helpful to him. "He would woo you, curry favor with you, and then when he no longer needed you, you would be dropped like a hot potato," she said.

Could he make it today?

"Today's corporation chief executives are different; they know more about public relations. And today's important

n't as flashy or as free-wheeling as they were a gen-
or two ago. But I think Ben could certainly make it
There are always people who follow the piper who gives
ise of making them realize their dreams, as he did for all
t.. se people in the past. Whether he could succeed to the extent that he did then is hard to say. It is more restrictive these
days, with tougher stockholders, consumers, and media.

"Ben was really the last of the flash-in-the-pan press
agents. But he had a lot more. He was a genius in his own
way, a genius at plowing the area he was in. There are lots of
press agents, but there was never one with his flair. He probably would have made a great actor. But, in a negative way,
he was an example of what not to be. His principles and procedures have not been emulated. He would never be considered someone of high ethics. No serious public-relations
practitioner would emulate him. He was a manipulator. We
all do some of that, but he did it all the time. He was totally
one-directional. Public relations these days is a management
function on a par with other management functions like finance, marketing, strategic planning. Public relations evalu-
ates public attitudes. It identifies the policies and procedures
of an individual or an organization with the public interest
and it plans and executes a program of action to earn public
understanding and acceptance. Publicity is a very important
part of it, but it must follow a policy set by management. Ben
reversed that, making publicity a matter of priority. He set
his own policy, and because he was so good they let him do
that."

She paused and added, "I guess I know more public-relations people in the world than anyone does but, with all his
faults, Ben was incomparable at what he did and what he un-
dertook to do. He was the outstanding publicist of his time. I
am sorry that he is gone because with him went color, charm
and fascination."

The other individual approached was Alistair Cooke, Ben's
longtime friend and the historian and host for the "Master-
piece Theater" on the Public Broadcasting Network.

In his soft-spoken, well-articulated way, Alistair Cooke
gave this summing up:

"If for some thirty years you see someone twice a week,
you can get to know him pretty well, and it was possible for

me to know Ben very well. But—and I speak as a reporter on the road for so many years in every state of the union, covering every conceivable kind of story and every conceivable type of American—he remains the most memorable American I ever met."

After these two appraisals, anything else is probably superfluous. He was truly one of a kind, and, for better or worse, his like probably will not be seen again.

BIBLIOGRAPHY

Bird, Robert S. "Luckman, Still Salesman of Brains." *New York Herald Tribune*. August 1, 1955.

———. "Luckman's Fabulous Career—Soap to Architecture." *New York Herald Tribune*. July 31, 1955.

Brady, James. "An Unpublished N.Y. Obituary." *Advertising Age*. October 9, 1978.

Calta, Louis. "250 First-Nighters Take Over Sonnenberg's Home for a Party." *New York Times*. November 15, 1967.

Cooke, Alistair. "The House of Sonnenberg." *Parke-Bernet Catalog*. June 1979.

"Corporations, Old Empire, New Prince." *Time* magazine. June 10, 1945.

Ennis, Thomas W. "Wealthy Group Saves Gramercy Park Landmark." *New York Times*. January 20, 1967.

Gill, Brendan. "An Alabaster Egg . . ." *New York Times*. August 8, 1979.

———. "Number Nineteen Gramercy Park." *Catalog of the Morgan Library's Sonnenberg Collection*. Preface by Charles Ryskamp, director. 1971.

Goldberger, Paul. "First Visit to a Grand New York Home." *New York Times.* December 21, 1978.

———. "The Last Town House." *Esquire* magazine. March 13, 1979.

Hellman, Geoffrey. "A House on Gramercy Park." *The New Yorker.* April 8, 1950.

"Lillian Wald of Henry Street." *Industrial Bulletin.* August 1965.

"Noted Gramercy Park Antique Collection Will Be Sold During Auction in June." *Town & Village.* May 17, 1979.

Phillips, McCandlish. "Henry Street Losing a Friend of 34 Years' Standing." *New York Times.* June 13, 1967.

Reif, Rita. "Record Sonnenberg Art Sale Opening." *New York Times.* June 5, 1979.

Runyon, Damon. "The Brighter Side—the House that Hot Air Built." *Chicago Herald-American.* May 11, 1946.

Sonnenberg, Ben. "Lost Property." *Grand Street.* Winter 1982.

———. "Lost Property." *The Nation.* June 30, 1979.

"Sonnenberg Takes Historic Property." *New York Times.* April 3, 1945.

INDEX